Empowerment and Autonomy of Women

Empowerment and Autonomy of Women

Ushirika wa Neema Deaconess Centre in the
Evangelical Lutheran Church in Tanzania,
Northern Diocese

Godrick Efraim Lyimo

FOREWORD BY
Aud V. Tønnessen

RESOURCE *Publications* · Eugene, Oregon

EMPOWERMENT AND AUTONOMY OF WOMEN
Ushirika wa Neema Deaconess Centre in the Evangelical Lutheran Church in Tanzania, Northern Diocese

Copyright © 2016 Godrick Efraim Lyimo. All rights reserved. Except for brief quotations in critical publications or reviews, no part of this book may be reproduced in any manner without prior written permission from the publisher. Write: Permissions, Wipf and Stock Publishers, 199 W. 8th Ave., Suite 3, Eugene, OR 97401.

Resource Publications
An Imprint of Wipf and Stock Publishers
199 W. 8th Ave., Suite 3
Eugene, OR 97401

www.wipfandstock.com

PAPERBACK ISBN: 978-1-4982-8447-9
HARDCOVER ISBN: 978-1-4982-8449-3
EBOOK ISBN: 978-1-4982-8448-6

Manufactured in the U.S.A.

This book is dedicated to my wife, Edda Kway Lyimo, my daughter, Faith, My son Nathaniel and my parents, whose prayers, encouragement and love made this work successful.

Contents

List of Tables and Figures | viii
Foreword | ix
Preface | xi
Acknowledgement | xiii
List of Abbreviations | xv

1. Introduction | 1
2. Women and Gender Issues | 9
3. Understanding the Context: The Chagga People of Kilimanjaro | 25
4. History of *Ushirika wa Neema* Deaconess Ministry | 39
5. Third-Wave Feminism and Empowerment Theory | 64
6. The Empowerment of Women by *Ushirika wa Neema* Deaconesses Centre | 88
7. Summary, Conclusion and Recommendations | 129

Appendix 1: History of the Evangelical Lutheran Church in Tanzania | 137
Appendix 2: Testimony of the First Missionaries at *Ushirika wa Neema* | 139

Bibliography | 143

Tables

Table 1: Educational progress of deaconesses at *Ushirika wa Neema* | 112

Table 2: List of courses pursued by deaconesses in various colleges | 112

Figures

Figure 1: The Three Dimensions of Empowerment | 74

Foreword

WOMEN CONSTITUTE HALF OF the population in the world, but power is not distributed evenly according to numbers and rather unevenly according to gender. Empowering women means enabling them to take up responsibility and to broaden their competence and capacity. It means utilizing resources which are often overlooked and neglected. The Christian Church has a history of male dominance, however as argued in this book by Godrick Efraim Lyimo, the Church has recently provided women with new opportunities to explore their talents and given them a platform wherefrom to act with empowerment in their service for Christ and the community.

One such historically important example is the protestant deaconess movement that was established in Germany in the late 19th Century. Then it was exported to other countries, and Lyimo presents the history of the Ushirika wa Neema Deaconess Centre of the ELCT-Northern Diocese. The centre was established in 1980 with the assistance of German deaconesses, and Lyimo gives the first academic account of its history, work and impact. It is an inspiring and challenging history Lyimo reveals. Empowering women within the structures of the Deaconess Centre has increased women´s agencies at home and strengthen their contribution in family care.

Foreword

At the same time such empowerment has been challenged by Chagga patriarchal traditions. Lyimo provides us with plenty of examples of how women in clever ways have negotiated between oppressive traditions and new-won competence and skills. He also shows how young deaconesses have to face the risks of stigmatization due to the demand of a celibate life style, as this contradicts basic values and norms in their Chagga culture, where marriage and motherhood are held in the highest esteem.

Lyimo has written a well informed book that I hope will be read by many and inspire even more to see the blessings of empowering women.

Aud V. Tønnessen

Professor in Church History Faculty
of Theology—University of Oslo

Preface

THE MAIN AIM OF this book is to explore how Ushirika wa Neema Deaconess Centre contributes to the empowerment of women in the Evangelical Lutheran Church in Tanzania (ELCT)-Northern Diocese and fosters gender awareness in the church and the entire community. It also explores challenges which the deaconesses face in the Chagga patriarchal society. This book is based on the research that was submitted to the Faculty of Theology of the University of Oslo as a requirement for the award of the degree of Masters of theology.

The theoretical framework consists of Third Wave Feminist views of empowerment. The focus was on women's empowerment which enables women to be critical and conscious about external realities and provides an awareness about their internal thought construction and belief systems that affect their well being in terms of gender, social justice, as well as the determination to use their physical, intellectual, emotional, and spiritual resources to protect their lives and sustain values that guarantee gender equality at the personal, social, economic and institutional level.

Ushirika wa Neema Deaconess Centre provides women with opportunities, such as the means for independent income, for education, for professional training and for learning skills. These opportunities change women's self-esteem, as well as raise their self-confidence and respect in the church and community. Women's agency at home increased to some extent because of engaging in income-generating activities. Thus, women's agency helps women to give advice to family members on different issues and influence household decisions. In addition, the education offered to deaconesses at Ushirika wa Neema has contributed to enable women to qualify as leaders in different institutions in the ELCT-Northern Diocese. Deaconesses in leadership positions practice participatory and inclusive leadership which includes collaboration and teamwork. This contributes to changing the mindset of the Chagga patriarchal society so that women can be better leaders like, or more than, men.

Moreover, there is a tension between Chagga cultural values and the celibate life style of the deaconesses at Ushirika wa Neema which directly counters Chagga traditional social values of marriage and child-bearing. It is evident that the learning of different skills at Ushirika wa Neema makes women more independent and self-reliant. From the findings of the study, it has been recommended that strategies and mechanisms for gender equality must be strengthened.

Acknowledgments

FOREMOST, I WOULD LIKE to thank the Almighty God for His gracious help and guidance in writing this book. This book is a revised form of my Master's thesis which I did in Norway at Oslo University (UIO) from 2011 to 2013. Therefore, there are many people I want to thank for giving advice, guidance and support during the writing of this book.

I would like to thank my supervisor, Professor Aud Tønnessen from the faculty of Theology, University of Oslo for her support and encouragement. Her questions, comments, wise insights and guidance helped me to accomplish this book.

My deepest gratitude is extended to Bishop Dr. Shoo, retired Bishops: Dr. Shao, Dr. Kweka, Mother of Deaconesses, Chaplain of *Ushirika wa Neema* and Sr. Dietlinde from Mother House in Augsburg, Germany, for providing me with information for the development of this book.

I would like also to thank all informants and deaconesses at Ushirika wa Neema for their information, which helped me to accomplish this study. I appreciate their help and transparency during the interviews. I also acknowledge, with deep thanks, the Norwegian State Education Loan Fund (*Lanekassen*) for financial support to enable this work to come into being.

Last, but not least, thanks are directed to my wife, Edda, and our daughter, Faith, who tolerated my long absence from home. They missed my fatherly love during the time when I was preparing this book.

Abbreviations

AD	Anno Domini
AIDS	Acquired Immunodeficiency Syndrome
CEDAW	Convention on the Elimination of All Forms of Discrimination against Women
DAWN	Development Alternatives with Women for a New Era
Dr.	Doctor
ELCT	Evangelical Lutheran Church in Tanzania
GDP	Gross Domestic Product
GAD	Gender and Development
HIV	Human Immunodeficiency Virus
IMF	International Monetary Fund
KCMC	Kilimanjaro Christian Medical Centre
LWF	Lutheran World Federation
LDC	Less Developed Country
MWCD	Ministry of Women and Child Development
ND	Northern Diocese
NCW	National Commission for Women

Abbreviations

NGOs	Non-Governmental Organizations
UN	United Nations
Rev	Reverend
Sr	Sister
SMMUCo	Stefano Moshi Memorial University College
TAMWA	Tanzanian Media Women Association
TGNP	Tanzania Gender Network Programme
UNFPA	United Nations Population Fund
UWN	Ushirika wa Neema
UK	United Kingdom
UCB	Uchumi Commercial Banks
UWT	Union of Women in Tanzania
WCC	World Council of Churches
WILA	Women in Development and Law
WID	Women in Development
WB	World Bank
Yrs	Years

CHAPTER 1

Introduction

Background and Motivation

THE EMANCIPATION AND EMPOWERMENT of women has been a worldwide phenomenon of concern to many countries and organizations within the twentieth and twenty-first centuries. Although Tanzania as a country and the Evangelical Lutheran Church in Tanzania–Northern Diocese (ELCT-ND) as an institution have embraced the idea of gender equality, most women in Tanzania have yet to experience this in full. This book is, therefore, based upon an understanding of the church as participating in God's mission which is rooted in a context of equality and as such stands in a better position to empower women to overcome some of the patriarchal practices that have put them on the margin of attaining full humanity. Therefore, the book will examine how ELCT-ND through Ushirika wa Neema Deaconess Centre empowers women and influences gender awareness in the church and society.

Women's empowerment seeks to enable women to identify their potential and contribute to the life of church and society. Empowerment influences many changes in women's lives, such as access to income, education and professional jobs, which increase their contribution and participation in the church and society. However, Tanzanian women, like many other women in the world, continue to struggle for economic, social, political and spiritual empowerment in order to get rid of oppressive patriarchal

Empowerment and Autonomy of Women

cultures. As Oduyoye[1] argues, within many relationships in which African women engage, she is placed at a lower level due to the hierarchies of patriarchy. This accord with Fiorenza[2] who argues that the status of women even in the churches which ordain women is still low compared to her male counterpart within an oppressive patriarchal structure. Therefore, women are often disempowered; thus, women's empowerment is a vital tool to promote positive change in women's lives.

The Diocese has put much effort addressing women's concerns in the church and society. The empowerment of women has been an important topic in the ELCT-ND. The Diocese has declared its desire to participate in the global efforts that address women's concerns and tackle sources of oppression and discrimination. This decision was made in the general assembly meeting of the ELCT in 2009, which affirmed the promotion of women's empowerment in order to influence gender equality in the church and society. In line with this argument, Oduyoye[3] argues that women's empowerment is a vital aspect to foster mutual relationships because God created women and men equally human, made them stewards of creation and gave them authority to manage it jointly.

Ushirika wa Neema (UWN) Deaconess Centre is one among the institutions used by the Northern Diocese to promote women's empowerment. It offers women opportunities to become deaconesses. They work among the women in the diocese. Therefore, this book seeks to investigate how Ushirika wa Neema Deaconess Centre contributes to the empowerment of women in the Diocese. In order to do this, I will study the work they do and discuss in what ways this contributes to the empowerment of women in the deaconess movement, as well as women who are assisted by them. The deaconess centre is historically new in the history of the ELCT-ND. I will therefore also examine the history of deaconess ministry in the diocese and especially look at the motivations behind it. Was the issue of empowerment part of the motivation?

1. Oduyoye, *Who Will Roll the Stone Away?* 22.
2. Fiorenza, "Waiting-at-Table" 315–16.
3. Oduyoye, *Who Will Roll the Stone Away?* 12.

Introduction

And I will identify and discuss challenges which face deaconesses in Chagga patriarchal society.

In 2010 I was invited to preach at Ushirika wa Neema deaconess chapel. After the sermon, the chaplain shared with me how both deaconesses are practicing diaconal services to the community as well as all the activities they are engaging in. He showed me some projects which are conducted by Ushirika wa Neema Deaconess Centre. These projects include domestic agriculture, animal keeping and the Montessori Kindergarten College. He further explained how women from different parishes visit the Centre in order to learn various life skills which improve their standard of living. Since then I developed an interest to learn how Ushirika wa Neema Deaconess Centre can contribute to the empowerment of women in the church and society. As Bryman states, "Academics conduct social research because there is development in society that provides an interest point of departure for the investigation of what is going on in the society."[4] I asked the chaplain to lend me a book on deaconess ministry in the Evangelical Lutheran Church in Tanzania—Northern Diocese so that I could learn more about their contribution to women's empowerment. Unfortunately he had no book about the Ushirika wa Neema Deaconess Centre. I decided to go to the Christian Bookshop which is owned by deaconesses and look for any published book on the deaconess ministry in Evangelical Lutheran Church in Tanzania—Northern Diocese. I didn't find any book on this theme. This motivated me to explore how Ushirika wa Neema can contribute to the empowerment of women in the Diocese and their history in order to document it and make it known to people in the church and community. It will be useful for both the current and the future generations to know the contribution of Ushirika wa Neema to the women's empowerment as well as origin of the deaconess ministry in the Evangelical Lutheran Church in Tanzania—Northern Diocese.

---

4. Bryman, *Social Research Methods*, 5.

Purpose and significance

The main purpose of this book is to investigate how Ushirika wa Neema Deaconess Centre contributes to the empowerment of women in the Evangelical Lutheran Church in Tanzania—Northern Diocese. In order to address this purpose, the book also explored the origin and formation of the deaconess ministry in the Evangelical Lutheran Church in Tanzania—Northern Diocese and analyzed the challenges which deaconesses at Ushirika wa Neema face in the Chagga patriarchal society. To reach that purpose I have developed the following objectives: First, to explore how the Ushirika wa Neema Deaconess Centre contributes to the empowerment of women in the Evangelical Lutheran Church in Tanzania –Northern Diocese. I am especially concerned with the work they perform and the way they engage in the local community in order to facilitate the empowerment of women within the movement as well as in the local community. Second, to examines the history of the deaconess ministry in the Evangelical Lutheran Church in Tanzania—Northern Diocese. Here I emphasize the motivations behind the establishment of the Ushirika wa Neema with regard to the issue of empowerment of women. The focus will be on how the issue of empowerment of women play a role in the establishment of the centre. Third, to examines the challenges which the deaconesses at Ushirika wa Neema face in the Chagga patriarchal society. Although the deaconess centre has been supported by the church, it is also clear that the work of the centre and the empowerment of women could be seen by some as being in conflict with cultural traditions and social practices in the Chagga society, especially with regard to the more patriarchal habits and attitudes.

This book is important because of the following: first, it explores the contribution of deaconesses to the empowerment of women in the church and society. This might be useful to church leaders, to promote women's empowerment, because the Evangelical Lutheran Church in Tanzania declared in her conference in 2009 to address the issue of gender equality. Second, it raises more awareness for government leaders concerning gender issues as they also declared that gender is a sensitive issue for the development of Tanzania. This book will facilitate more promotion of women to education in secondary schools and colleges, an issue which the government has started implementing, compared to previous times where priority was given to boys only. Third, it contributes to new knowledge about the origin and formation of the deaconess ministry in the Evangelical Lutheran Church in Tanzania—Northern Diocese. Fourth, the book is intended to help the women themselves, the church, informants and the society to understand the contemporary empowerment of women and the rapid changes of gender relations in every state of human life. This book is valuable to the readers as well as the entire church to learn how women respond to their contemporary challenges in a patriarchal society, such as challenging oppressive structures in church and community. Also, they will study how education offered at Ushirika wa Neema may be a vital tool for awakening women conscietization and consciousness, which are the fundamental factors in influencing gender awareness and empowerment of women in the society and church.

Generally, the book strongly calls all church authorities and governmental leaders to promote the empowerment of women in Tanzania and the world at large. Specifically in rural areas, where patriarchal cultures are still active, there is a need to continue teaching people to accommodate women leaders into their social structure and change the cultural concept that women are not leaders but are just custodians of the family. They should be helped to recognize the potential contribution of women leaders in their society.

Theoretical Framework and Methodology

In order to accomplish the writing of this book, it was necessary to employ feminist theoretical perspectives. I found it useful to apply the so-called Third-Wave Feminism which is concerned with how women are empowered and enabled to have new self-understanding of their value and roles. They see themselves as independent.

Third-Wave feminism is a feminist movement that began in the 1990s to the present. It involves economic, political, social, and personal empowerment of women. Also, it focuses more on the individual empowerment of women than on activism. It promotes women to build meaningful identities in the complex contemporary world. Therefore, I will use this theory to find out if the work of deaconesses at Ushirika wa Neema contributes to an increased independency of women, both those who work as deaconesses and those who are assisted by them. However, I look at it from different perspectives such as economical, social and family. More detail information and concepts of so-called Third-Wave Feminism and the empowerment theories are discussed in chapter five.

Since little is written about the history of Ushirika wa Neema and there are few written sources that explain the work and motivation of the centre, I have chosen a qualitative research method based on interviews. This gave me the opportunity to learn both what the deaconesses do and how their work is understood by people involved in it and close observers of it.

The study employed the qualitative research strategy because the goal of qualitative research is to understand a particular social situation, event, role, group or interaction. In line with this argument, Marshal[5] affirms that qualitative research fosters engagement in everyday life between researcher and respondents. The researcher interacts with respondents and acquires significant information.

The data obtained from the field is not usually expressed in numerical terms. This does not mean that numerical figures are never used in this study, but most of the data is qualitative. That is to say, most of the analysis is done by description or word.[6] On the other hand, Creswell points out some important features of qualitative research as follows: qualitative research usually takes place in a natural setting in which both human behaviour and events happen.[7] The vital aim of qualitative research is to solicit participants'

---

5. Marshal et al, *Qualitative Research*, 24.
6. Bryman, *Social Research Methods*, chapter 2.
7. Creswell, *Research Design*, 56.

INTRODUCTION

perceptions, experiences, and the way they make sense of their lives. It focuses on the understanding of various realities. It also focuses on how phenomena occur in various discourses.

Therefore, this strategy helped me to interact with the participants within the study and ask them questions in order to get a deeper meaning of specific issues regarding the empowerment of women and deaconess sisters' ministry in Tanzania. Since little is written on establishment of deaconess sisters and how they promote the empowerment of women in the Tanzanian context, this strategy helped me to acquire significant insights from deaconess sisters, women, pastors and bishops.

Moreover, I used the interview method for collecting data because it favours face-to-face contact and conversation with the respondents. This method allowed the use of guiding questions as I prepared them for interviews. The method has an added advantage as it allowed me to substitute and reframe the questions and elaborate where they were not clearly understood. It also enabled me to ask more questions from the respondent's information in order to get detailed information on the topic under study. Documentary analysis was also considered but little is written on the deaconess ministry in ECT-Northern Diocese. Only a few reports and documents collected from the field discuss the role of the deaconesses in relation to marginalized people in the community. This situation required me to depend more on oral interviews which enabled me to acquire detailed information and reflections of the interviewees on the topic under study.

Structure and Synopsis

In order to present the argument of this book, I have structured it into seven chapters. The first chapter provides the introduction, background of the book, motivation of writing this book, significance of the book, and the objectives of the book. Chapter two discusses Women and gender issues in the church and society. Chapter three presents the background information about Chagga people in Kilimanjaro–Tanzania. Chapter four presents the history of the deaconess ministry. Chapter five discusses theoretical approaches to feminism and women's empowerment. Chapter six discusses the empowerment of women by Ushirika wa Neema deaconess centre. Lastly, chapter seven presents the conclusion and recommendations. This synopsis of the chapters is important because it enables the readers to understand the coherent of the contents of this book. I concluded my discussions in this book by proposing some areas that need further investigation regarding the empowerment of women in our modern time.

CHAPTER 2

Women and Gender Issues

Introduction

THE FOCUS OF THIS book is to examine how Ushirika wa Neema Deaconess centre promotes the empowerment of women in Tanzanian context. Therefore, I find it essential to start with some discussion on women and gender issues in the church and society. This chapter will enable the readers to learn how women in a patriarchal society suffer violence and oppression of many kinds that are legitimized by both religions and the societies of which they are a part. Religions sometimes oppress women by applying some biblical patriarchal traditions. Women are still considered as the property of men. In many African societies, whether patriarchal or matrilineal, gender hierarchy and male supremacy subordinated women to men.

The chapter will begin by discussing gender issues in the Tanzanian context. In this section, I will show the challenges facing women and female pastors as well as approaches used by women to overcome them. The next subsection examines gender inequality. Under gender inequality, I explored how women are still relegated to inferior status in economic, political, social, intellectual and religious spheres. Furthermore, the chapter indicates how the patriarchal system is at work in family relationships and has been mirrored in the structure of the church and society. In many African societies, women have not been elevated to leadership positions and high levels of decision-making processes and governance whether in church or society.

Gender Issues in the Tanzanian Context

There is not much written about the Ushirika wa Neema Deaconess Centre, but there are relevant research studies of the church in Tanzania from many critical perspectives on gender. One such researches is by Kurubai Rebecca[1] who conducted a master's research entitled "From Doubt to Acceptance: The Coming of Women into Clerical Ministry in the Evangelical Lutheran Church in Tanzania." She focused on women's ordination in the Evangelical Lutheran Church in Tanzania in comparison with women's ordination experience in other parts of the world such as the Norwegian Lutheran State Church, the Evangelical Lutheran Church of Finland and the Evangelical Lutheran Church of America. She discussed mainly the role and challenges facing women pastors as well as approaches used by women pastors to overcome them. Concerning the challenges, her study identified family as a challenge in the sense that male pastors were found to have less family challenges compared to female pastors. The rationale for this was that in patriarchal society, women are responsible for taking care of the children and domestic activities. Therefore, male pastors do not participate in taking care of their children and domestic activities; their wives look after them. Kurubai's study shows that female pastors have double burdens. They are responsible for both domestic activities and parish duties. Sometimes female pastors are assigned to work in difficult parishes and once they become pregnant, they suffer so much due to working too much in the home and at the parish, all of which require walking long distances. After their babies are born, they are sometimes compelled to shorten their maternity leave in order to continue with pastoral responsibilities. Moreover, the study revealed that there is a tension between male and female pastors. Some men have difficulty in accepting female pastors, and

---

1. Kurubai, *From Doubt to Acceptance*, 10–55.

when they see a female pastor with confidence and authority in her leadership position, sometimes they find ways to put her down and discourage her so that people can say she cannot lead.[2] This implies that in a patriarchal society, female pastors find various challenges in their ministries because of the patriarchal practices which undermine women. In such situations, female pastors need to be strong with self-confidence and self-esteem as well as hard-working in order to change the mindset of such men to know that women can be church ministers like men.

The study indicated that in order to overcome those challenges, female pastors in the Evangelical Lutheran Church in Tanzania—Northern Diocese have established an association which has been useful for female pastors to discuss different solutions to their challenges. Also, the association is used to comfort and encourage female pastors.

Though this study does not address the role of deaconess, Kurubai discussed the problem which is relevant to this study, namely the challenges that many women face within a church that is male-dominated. Female pastors might be said to challenge the power of male leaders in more direct ways than deaconesses. Female pastors seek influence and power through direct competition with men, whereas deaconesses are placed in a different structure. However, the issue of gendered power and empowerment is common in these studies.[3]

Another Master's thesis by Chamshama Rhoda[4] is entitled "Prostitution, Culture and Church: A Study of Gender Inequality in Chalinze, Tanzania". Her study revealed that gender inequality in society was seen to be the core source for prostitution. Therefore, it suggested that to solve the challenge of prostitution, there is a need to confront the unjust social structures in Chalinze, Tanzania. She also noted that the church seems to concur with unjust structures in the society. It has been noted that the interpretations of some biblical texts in Chalinze local churches have been used

2. Ibid.
3. Ibid.
4. Rhoda, *Prostitution, Culture and Church*, 20–26.

to legitimate women's subordination to men and hence violence against them. These biblical texts seem to be interpreted in a way that empower the oppressive cultural structures, which violate women's rights. Moreover, the study revealed that many decisions in Tanzania, including decisions about women's own lives, are made by men. She states:

> Men are decision makers in many aspects. Women for instance, are not given chance to speak up, especially in the traditional meetings . . . if a woman happen to speak in traditional meetings, all people, including her fellow women get surprised . . . there is social-psychological discrimination against women in many society. Since this situation has lasted for quite a long time, it has become a norm, and as a result, the oppressed group seems to oppress itself.[5]

Thus, male supremacy in many societies in Tanzania seemed to undermine women in the traditional meetings. The majority of Women are kept out of the traditional and religious leadership; they do not participate in the same level as men. In the same vein, Oduyoye argues that in most parts of Africa, women are still considered as the property of men.[6] She noted that in many African societies, whether patriarchal or matrilineal, gender hierarchy and male supremacy subordinated women to men. In Chagga patriarchal society men are dominant in private and public life of women. On the other hand, Rhoda points out those Tanzanian women have formed organizations aimed at liberating women from all sources of oppressive practices. These organizations include Tanzania Gender Networking Programme (TGNP) and Tanzania Media Women's Association (TAMWA). They are playing a great role in opposing the way media negatively portray women in the media. They focus on educating and promoting gender awareness in Tanzania by helping both men and women to know their rights, with special attention given to women's and children's rights. In an innovative and strategic way, these organizations collaborate

---

5. Ibid.
6. Oduyoye, *Who Will Roll the Stone Away?* 30–45.

with journalists and use radio, television, newspapers, workshops and outreach activities to advocate issues which affect the lives of women and children such as HIV/AIDS, rape, wife battering, killing of elderly women due to misguided witchcraft beliefs and discrimination against women in decision-making.[7]

Therefore, one can argue that these organizations seem to change the situation of women in Tanzania, especially in towns. To some extent women have started to know their rights, and some men have started to recognize women's rights. Though these organizations have begun operating actively in the towns, they have not addressed the marginalized women in villages who are living vulnerable lives and have more problems. They need to expand their services to villages where women do not have access to television and radio. However, Ushirika wa Neema Deaconess Centre works with women from both town and village parishes. This aspect will be discussed in detail in chapter six.

Moreover, Ballington et al published a book *Tanzania Gender Observer Mission Report*.[8] In this book, authors indicated that women's movement in Tanzania has a long history. Since the 1950s, women have contributed to the national liberation struggle and were in the front line in promoting the struggle for independence against British Colonial rule. During that time, there was no clear feminist agenda, but a space was created for women to collaborate in independence activities.

Generally, this section indicates that male supremacy in many societies in Tanzania seemed to undermine women in different spheres including the traditional meetings and leadership, preventing women from participating in the same level as men. This attitude led to gender inequality as discussed.

---

7. Rhoda, *Prostitution, Culture and Church*, 78.
8. Ballington et al, *Tanzania Gender Observer Mission Report* 45.

Empowerment and Autonomy of Women

Gender Inequality

This subsection discusses gender inequality in various aspects of the church. The membership of the Evangelical Lutheran Church in Tanzania constitutes of more than 50% women.[9] The number of these women has neither been reflected in leadership positions and high level of decision-making nor in governance, whether in the church or society. For example, in the Executive Council of the Church, which is the next highest decision-making body to the General Assembly of ELCT, amongst its fifty-two members, five are women, which does not reflect their membership and contribution to the general growth of the church. In other decision-making organs of the ELCT like church councils in the district and parishes, women constitute less than 20%.[10] However, their work in church activities is very visible at the congregational level. They are the ones who oversee the kindergarten and Montessori nursery schools that are owned by the parishes.

The trend of imbalance can as well be traced in the educational sector. The enrolment of women in theological colleges is low compared to men. Theological education plays an important role in raising women's awareness against patriarchal oppression.[11] Generally, theological education is crucial as an initial catalyst of feminist theology. Therefore, the low enrolment of women into ELTC's theological seminaries aggravates the gender gap within the church leadership. Furthermore, when women are empowered theologically, gender equality flourishes more through formal and informal network including women and men working at a grassroots level in opposing those patriarchal cultures which oppress them. For example, women cannot decide on the number of children in the family though they are the ones playing a big role in child upbringing. Moreover, in Tanzania, it is estimated that women, especially rural women, provide 80 percent of the labour

---

9. www.elct.org/social.html. Retrieved on 28.09.2012.
10 Ibid.
11. King, *Feminist Theology from Third World*, 5.

force in rural areas and are producing 60 percent of food yield.[12] Though they are the main producers of cash and food crops, the environment does not allow them to own their own wealth. Their husbands are controllers of their income.

Women are still relegated to "inferior status in economic, political, social, intellectual and religious spheres. Their numbers have not been reflected in leadership positions and high levels of decision-making processes and governance whether in church or society".[13] The church should respond to the current plight of women economically, socially, politically and spiritually. The services of the church have to be extended to all and it should openly challenge the structures that hinder women from attaining the dignity that was theirs, equal to men at creation.

Phiri in her work *Women, Presbyterianism and Patriarchy* focuses on cultural hindrances, especially patriarchy, as a major setback for women in assuming leadership positions in the church and society.[14] Women are human beings like men, and they have intellect and ability to do different activities like men.[15] They have the intelligence and capability to lead the society, as Oduyoye argues that women are very good administrators because they learn at their very tender age how to organize everyday life.[16]

In Africa, as stated by Mwaura, "women form 80% of believers, yet are usually absent from its decision-making bodies."[17] The WCC Report on the Results of Mid-Ecumenical Decade of Churches in Solidarity with Women (1994–1996) as cited by Mwaura observes that women all over the world are the pillars of the church and are the majority in most congregations. They are active, participating strongly in the spiritual and liturgical life of the church's mission. However, many churches have failed to

---

12. Online at http://www.tanzania.go.tz/gender.html.
13. Mwaura, "Empowerment of Women," 28.
14. Phiri, "Doing Theology as an African Woman" 21.
15. Oduyoye, *The Will to Rise* 16.
16. Ibid.
17. Mwaura, "Empowerment of Women," 32.

receive and respond fully to women's gifts and admit them in the key areas of participation.[18]

Pemberton says that all women in a patriarchal society suffer violence and oppression of many kinds that are legitimized by both religions and societies of which they are a part. Religions sometimes oppress women by applying some biblical patriarchal traditions.[19] In support of this view, African feminist theologians like Oduyoye and Kanyoro argue those women have been oppressed by biblical traditions, which have a patriarchal setting. In Africa women have been made quiet by the patriarchal system.[20] In line with this argument, Fiorenza affirms:

> Since the political and religion right recognizes that women's anger and fear constitute a potential revolutionary force when directed against patriarchal institutions, it manipulates these fears by quieting and redirecting them. They then employ biblical religion to inculcate the subordination. Women can fulfil their feminine vocation by living the ideal of true complementarities. The Christian right offers women the love of Jesus, the perfect man, the one man to whom they can submit absolutely without being sexually violated or abused. The power of Christ enables wilful women to become submissive in the Lord so that they can subordinate themselves to the leadership of their husbands.[21]

Therefore, the patriarchal systems in different religions lead to unequal social structure whereby men have greater power and authority over women. This domination of women in religion is cemented also with African tradition religion.

The patriarchal system has also been influenced by the African religion which is tied with culture. As Oduyoye argues, "It must never be forgotten that culture and religion are significant within African life that neither Muslim nor Christian in Africa can be

---

18. Ibid.
19. Pemberton, *Circle Thinking*, 126.
20. Oduyoye and Kanyoro, *The Will to Rise: Women Traditions*, 57.
21. Fiorenza, *Discipleship of Equals*, 315.

totally free of the values that emanate from the traditional African Religion[22]". However, women's oppression is not only practiced in African religion but also in Christianity through biblical interpretation and Christian theology as Oduyoye argues: "Unfortunately, Biblical interpretation and Christian theology in Africa have had the effect of marginalizing women experience."[23] She further argues that the Bible does reinforce the traditional socio-cultural oppression of women, and Christianity has converted the African people to a new religion without converting their culture.[24] Similarly, Esposito John[25] in his article *Introduction: Women, Religion, and Empowerment* states: "However different, the daughters of Abraham, Sarah and Hagar have inherited a religious legacy that is not only the product of divine revelation but also of human interpretation . . . overwhelmingly male and patriarchal . . . as a result the image of women has been shaped by patriarch as much as by revelation."[26] In Tanzania most women are experiencing above all torture and suffering which are influenced by the patriarchal system. How does the deaconess ministry in ELCT-Northern diocese empower women to get rid of these values of the patriarchal cultures? This will be discussed in chapter six and seven.

Gender and Deaconess Ministry

There are many studies of the Protestant deaconess movement, though not of Ushirika wa Neema. But the formation of many Protestant deaconess centres shares much of the same origin from the German deaconess movement. Some of those studies are: Riipinen analyzed the deaconess ministry in the context of the Lutheran church in the Philippines.[27] Rasche expounded her re-

22. Oduyoye, *Daughters of Anowa*, 12.
23. Ibid, 175.
24. Ibid.
25. Esposito, "Introduction to Women, Religion and empowerment," 290–96.
26. Ibid, p.295.
27. Riipinen, *Holy Deacones*, 12–18.

search in the Deaconess Sisters: Pioneer Professional Women in St. Louis—Evangelical Church in America.[28] Green conducted a research on *Responding to Secularization: The Deaconess Movement in Nineteenth-Century Sweden* and Markkola[29] researched *Gender and Vocation: Women, Religion and Social Change in Nordic Countries, 1830–1940*.[30]

However, the studies mentioned above have not particularly addressed the issue of women's empowerment but have been more concerned with understanding how *diakonia* is enacted through their mission and activities. While this book does not focus on this important work, the deaconess centre I am describing advocate for the women's empowerment which has many common features with those deaconess movements mentioned above. For example, an interesting article that discusses the early church's involvement in diaconical activities is by Elizabeth, S. Fiorenza.[31] In her article "Waiting at a Table: A Critical Feminist Theological Reflection on Diakonia" Fiorenza shows from a feminist perspective how women were given a secondary status in the church despite engaging in church activities. This aspect has to do with how women's status was constructed in various cultures and societies. She argues that because of gender inequality in the patriarchal church, women have been given auxiliary roles, secondary status in the ministry, and have not been involved in decision-making. She further argues that women perform a lot of church activities without having been paid. She states:

> Women engaged in such volunteer ministry or church works which are minimally paid if they are remunerated at all. Women engaged in such volunteer ministry are mostly middle-aged, middle-class married women whose children have left the home, who have no professional career, and whose husbands are able to support them. At the price of their continuing economic dependence they

---

28. Rasche, *The Deaconess Sisters*, 11.
29. Markkola, *The Calling of Women Gender*, 14.
30. Green, *Responding to Secularization*, 34.
31. Fiorenza, *Waiting-at-Table*, 83–90.

can afford ministry, whereas poor women and welfare mothers are not able to do so.[32]

The above statement shows that men practiced ministry with virtue of ordination and gained high status and remuneration, compared to the women who were engaging in voluntary ministry with no payment or minimal remuneration. In both churches and society, the majority of social, charitable volunteer workers are women. Even in the churches which allow women ordination, still there is ministerial inequality because the governing board and decision-making bodies are dominated by a patriarchal structure.

Patriarchy, Gender, and Power Relations

Before going any further, let me discuss the concepts of patriarchy in relation to gender and power relations within particular cultural orientations. The concept of culture containing a complexity of features and issues is essential in all communities. This complexity is definitely the case in the Tanzanian context. With regard to this complex society, this book is not focusing on providing a comprehensive account of all its cultural aspects. However, there are some aspects which are common in Tanzanian cultures which hamper the empowerment of women. One of the main aspects which hamper the empowerment of women in Tanzania and position is patriarchal culture. This argument is in line with Fischman who argues that patriarchal structures and male authority is the global phenomenon where the majority of men enjoy the privilege of the gender dividend.[33] However, patriarchy is a problematic term to analyze. Despite the challenges in defining the term, there have been multiple attempts, and King's definition could be a starting point: "The patriarchy is a social structure whereby men have greater power and authority over women and children. In patriarchal society men are considered as decision makers, leaders, and

---

32. Ibid, 83.
33. Fischman, *Imagining Teaches*, 25.

controller of the properties. In this discourse property and title are inherited by male lineage."[34]

King further insists that the patriarchal system is at work in family relationships and has been mirrored in the structure of the church and society. Women are often excluded from leadership and decision making, as well as and subordinated to men.[35] This agrees with Merriam-Webster who claims that patriarchy is a social system in which men are regarded as the authority within the family and society. Furthermore, societies can be based on a patriarchal system when "Social organization marked by the supremacy of the father in the clan or family, the legal dependence of wives and children, and the reckoning of descent and inheritance in the male line; broadly: control by men of a disproportionately large share of power a society or institution organized according to the principles or practices of patriarchy."[36]

From the above quote, one can argue that when one group in the society enjoys the privilege, another group is denied in enjoying the advantages of having that privilege. Since patriarchal culture is male–dominated, it tends to favor and offer privileges and opportunities to more men than women. However, there should be a mechanism which facilitates the division of power between men and women which needs to be examined.

The relationship between patriarchy and power is vital to be discussed. The analysis made by Lerner between patriarchy and power shows how patriarchal scholars constructed their structure which excluded women in the leadership. The majority of women are kept out of the patriarchal leadership structures. The explanation of how women are kept out is usually not even made explicit.[37] This implies that there is a hidden process of exclusion. Women are simply eliminated from the scene and marginalized silently. Lerner insists that religion, science, philosophy are the three great mental constructs which explain how the contribution of women

34. King, *Feminist Theology*, 39.
35. Ibid.
36. Merriam-Webster, *Patriarchy*, 3.
37. Lerner, *Why have there been so few Women*, 7.

are made invisible or silent.[38] The majority of Women are kept out of the science, philosophy, and religious leadership; they do not participate in the same level as men. This situation poses critical questions: Is there any natural division of power and privileges between men and women? Is there any other paramount reason rather than the mere biological differences between the men and women? Is power applied in an authoritarian manner, in the way that some people are seen as superior while others as inferior? This categorization fosters unequal distribution of power between men and women.

However, there are some evidences which show that the difference between men and women is beyond the biological factor. In this scenario, the concept of gender is relevant and plays a key role in this issue. Gender is a social construct grounded on the basis of the bodily differences between men and women. Bourdieu states:

> The social world constructs the body as a sexually defined reality and as the depository of sexually defining principles of vision and division. (. . .) The biological differences between sexes, i.e. between the male and female bodies, and in particular, the anatomical difference between the sex organs, can thus appear as the natural justification of the socially constructed difference between the genders, and in particular of the social division of labor.[39]

The above quote indicates that gender difference between men and women is biological. Other differences between female and male are social constructs which are created by our societies. Furthermore, gender can be defined as "a social–historical construction that affects and is affected by individual and social practices that are conscious and unconsciously exercised."[40] Gender is "Part of complex system of norms and values that is extremely influential in shaping the relationships between individuals of the same or

---

38. Ibid.
39. Bourdieu, *On Male Domination*, 11.
40. Fischman, *Imagining Teaches*, 25.

different sexes, between individuals and society, and between individuals and institutionalized structures of power."[41]

The quotation above means that gender is a set of qualities and behavior expected from a female or male by society, in which the respective roles are learned through socialization processes.[42] This aspect is in line with UNESCO which states:

> Gender is a social and cultural construct, which distinguishes differences in the attributes of men and women, and accordingly refers to the roles and responsibilities of men and women. Gender-based roles and other attributes, therefore, change over time and vary with different cultural contexts. The concept of gender includes the expectations held about the characteristics, aptitudes and likely behaviours of both women and men (femininity and masculinity). This concept is also useful in analyzing how commonly shared practices legitimize discrepancies between sexes.[43]

As stated in the quotation above, gender roles are constructed by the society and imparted from one person to another through socialization since the childhood. Wasa affirms this assertion:

> Men and women may inhabit considerably different social worlds in a society. If both men and women function as significant others in primary socialization, they mediate these discrepant realities to the child . . . the male and female version of reality are socially recognized, and this recognition, too, is transmitted in primary socialization . . . the child will know the version appertaining to the other sex . . . but he will not identify with this version.[44]

Therefore, gender is a social construct which is influenced by traditions and cultures in a particular society. Wasa comments that

---

41. Ibid.
42. Wasa, *Stranded between Tradition and Modernity*, 37.
43. UNESCO, *Gender in Education*, 25.
44. Wasa, *Stranded between Tradition and Modernity*, 37.

the focus on how patriarchal traditions and structures impact on women has foundations in a historical context.[45]

The above point of view is in agreement with Fischman as cited by Wasa who states: "Discourses about gender do not exist detached from social relations or in a historical vacuum. What is designated under the category of gender or what is considered a gender issue is not a straightforward reflection of the social and economic conditions of men and women, but gender is constructed within these conditions."[46]

Generally, gender identity is how a person considers herself/himself socially and how an individual interact with the world in her/his community. In other words, gender identity is how we define ourselves and the meaning it creates in our lives. It is important to note that the current society is experiencing changes which are promoting the empowerment of women in the church and society. These changes include the massive campaign from West and America which fosters female education, birth control, women rights, reform of laws, and sponsoring women projects. This new system of reconstruction of Tanzanian culture is weakening the patriarchal structures and recognizes women rights.

Conclusion

In this chapter, I have presented the contemporary situation of women and gender issues in Tanzania and Africa at large. I discussed also how women in a patriarchal society suffer violence and oppression of many kinds that are legitimized by both religions and societies of which they are a part. In this respect, the discussion has heighted how women have not been reflected in leadership positions and high levels of decision-making processes and governance whether in church or society. Women are often excluded from leadership and decision making and subordinated to men. Furthermore, the concept of gender is critically analyzed. The

---

45. Ibid.
46. Ibid., 37.

chapter indicated that gender roles are constructed by the society and imparted from one person to another through socialization since the childhood. Therefore, the government of Tanzania and Evangelical Lutheran Church in Tanzania are now emphasizing on construction of a democratic state which pay attention of gender issues. The next chapter analyzes the context in which the research was carried. This is useful to enable the reader to understand the context and be familiar with the culture of Chagga people of Kilimanjaro region in Tanzania.

CHAPTER 3

Understanding the Context

The Chagga People of Kilimanjaro in Tanzania

Introduction

THE DEACONESS CENTRE OF Ushirika wa Neema in Northern Diocese is situated at the slopes of Mountain Kilimanjaro, which are the inhabitation of the Chagga from time immemorial. Thus, I find it essential to start with a presentation of the Chagga tribe. Thereafter, I will provide the description of the Northern Diocese, a place where I carried out my research.

By presenting the historical overview of Chagga tribe and Northern Diocese with its people's socio-cultural life, the aim is to highlight and understand its culture with special emphasis on the role of gender and the gender power relations.

In this respect, the chapter will discuss women and gender issues in the Chagga tribe. Under this subsection the issue of inheritance of the land will be discussed in detail. Land is regarded as male property inherited patrilineally by males from males or transferred from males to males. Chagga cultures do not allow women to own and inherit land. Even, though the Chagga women are primary farmers. After discussing how women in the Chagga tribe are not allowed to own and inherit land, I will also discuss women and marriage in the Chagga tribe. The focus will be to show Chagga understanding of marriage and significance of having children. In the Chagga tribe marriage and bearing of the children is respected and considered as a way of continuing life from one generation to another generation. This culture contradicts to that of deaconess sisters who opt to live celibate lives. Finally, I will examine education and gender issues in the Chagga tribe, showing the challenges which face women to acquire education.

The Chagga People

The Chagga is a tribe that is located in the United Republic of Tanzania, on the slopes of Mount Kilimanjaro which is the highest mountain in Africa whose peak stands at 5,895 meters above the sea level.[1] The United Republic of Tanzania was formed by the union of two sovereign states, namely Tanganyika and Zanzibar. Tanganyika became a sovereign state on 9th December, 1961 and became a Republic the following year. Zanzibar became independent on 10th December, 1963 and the People's Republic of Zanzibar was established after the revolution of 12th January 1964. The two sovereign republics formed the United Republic of Tanzania on 26th April, 1964. The United Republic of Tanzania is the largest state in east and central Africa, after the Republic of Congo (formerly Zaire) (Bendera 1999:118). Tanzania is situated on the east coast of Africa and lies between one degree and eleven degrees south of the equator.

The Chagga people are also called Wachagga who lives in Tanzania. Traditionally, the Chagga belonged to different clans of different dialect (groups of people of common descent). These clans include the following: Wasiha, Wamachame, Wakibosho, Wauru, Wamochi, Wavunjo and Warombo ruled by *mangi's* (chiefs). The Chagga area was divided into independent chiefdoms. The chiefs sometimes warred with each other. Other times, they formed alliances to try to increase their power. After Tanzania won its

---

1. Husu, *Desire and Death*, 10–25.

independence in 1961, the system of chiefdoms was abolished throughout the country. The main language spoken by the Chagga people is *Kichagga*. The Chagga speak various dialects in different regions depending on the above-mentioned clans. However, the Chagga people can understand each other despite these dialectical differences.

Almost all Chagga people also speak Kiswahili, the national language in Tanzania. Kiswahili is the language of instruction in primary schools and is used in the work-place. English is the language of instruction in secondary schools and institutions of higher learning. Each Chagga family has its own homestead which is known as *kihamba* (the plural of this word is *vihamba*). In other words, *kihamba* is the land along the slope of mount Kilimanjaro where the Chagga live and grow bananas as their staple food. *Kihamba* land is owned by males and is only inherited by the sons when the father dies. Coffee, which is the main cash crop cultivated in *kihamba*, was also introduced in Kilimanjaro in the 1880s by German settlers.[2] Therefore, coffee and banana are the main crops cultivated on *kihamba* for consumption and business. This agrees with Fleisch who says, "Wachagga are efficient both in agricultural and business."[3] In the same line Husu says: "The (Chagga) are among East Africa's wealthiest and most educated people . . . they are also known for their adaptability. They were one of the first tribes in the area to convert to Christianity. This may have given them an advantage over other ethnic groups, as they had access to education and health care as Christians."[4] Kilimanjaro region has the highest concentration of secondary schools in Tanzania and highest enrolment rate. The Chagga are highly educated and the most economically successful ethnic group in Tanzania.[5]

Fertile soil at *vihamba* along the slopes of Mount Kilimanjaro attracted many people from different tribes to settle there. In the course of time, they formed a unity which is known as Chagga.

2. Ibid.
3. Fleisch, Pail. *Lutheran Beginning*, 45.
4. Husu, *Desire and Death*, 45.
5. Materu, *The Impact of Chagga Traditional Beliefs and Practices*, 5.

Some of them settled there as a way of getting rid of their enemies in the lowlands shows that Chagga people do not constitute ethnical homogeneity i.e. the Chagga people are a mixture of people with different ethnic origins. They are said to originate from the tribes surrounding the slope of Mount Kilimanjaro such as Kamba and Taita from Kenya, as well as Pare, Kahe and Sambaa from the plains surrounding Mount Kilimanjaro.[6] Other factors which led to migration to the slope of Mount Kilimanjaro include business, friendships and marriage.

The Chagga people live in community. There are four distinctive aspects that bind the individual in the framework of the community. These aspects are namely the clan, age group, blood pact (*mma*) and neighbourhood. These are regarded as the main communal ties that promote the unity of the community. These primal ties define an individual. Ernest Jaeschke and Laurent Magesa emphasize that, relationship is imperative. When people meet for the first time in the Chagga community, their greeting is used to determine how they relate to one another. This involves remembering their ancestors. For example, one could say, "My name is X, my grandfather was Y who was circumcised together with your grandfather" or "I was circumcised together with your uncle" etc. The communal life is the central aspect of one's identity as well as in relationship to others as explained above.[7]

The ELCT—Northern Diocese

E.L.C.T Northern Diocese had been established by Lutheran mission work from the Leipzig mission.[8] Germany sent missionaries who first settled at Nkwarungo Machame in Kilimanjaro region[9] in 1893. Thus, the Kilimanjaro Region is one of the twenty admin-

6. Maanga, *Religion and Worldview*, 11.

7. Jaeschke, *Bruno Gutmann*, 56–71, cf. Magesa, *African Religion*, 64.

8. See Appendix 1: The History of Evangelical Lutheran Church in Tanzania.

9. Online at http://www.arcworld.org/downloads/Christian-Evangelical-Lutheran-Tanzania-7YP.pdf.

istrative subdivisions in Tanzania mainland. It is located at the north eastern corner of Tanzania. The region occupies the slopes of Mount Kilimanjaro, whose peak stands at 5,895 meters above sea level, making it the highest in Africa. The Kilimanjaro Region has a population of 1.4 million and an area of 13,309 km, with a population density of 104 people per km, compared with the national average of 37 people per km. The highlands of Kilimanjaro are where most farming takes place which has a population density of over 350 people per sqkm. After their settlement at Nkwarungo, Lutherans spread out over Kilimanjaro and Arusha in the Northern part of Tanzania. Shao indicates that these missionaries were not alone in Kilimanjaro; they were working alongside Roman Catholic missionaries who had already been there since 1890.[10]

According to Materu, the meeting of Lutherans and Catholic missionaries in Kilimanjaro caused some misunderstanding and conflict among them due to the fact that each of them competed for the Kilimanjaro region with the desire to occupy as big an area as possible.[11] In this case, Sundkler indicates that "in 1894 the German administrator, Captain Johannes stepped in and divided the country (region) into separate Catholic and Lutheran regions, with each group agreeing to strict principles of non-interference in the other's territory."[12] However, the agreement of no-interference did not last long after the departure of the foreign missionaries. Lutherans explicitly made the mission of the church to expand in areas where there was no Lutheranism. It was very clearly stated in the church plans to make areas without Lutheran Christians, including areas dominated by the Catholic Church, as mission areas where Lutheran missionary services were to be concentrated.[13]

The missionaries established various social services in Northern Diocese, which included education, health services etc. In line with this concept, Mwaluko affirms: "Missionaries agencies have been engaged in education, health and social welfare development

---

10. Shao, *Bruno Gutman's Missionary Method*, 41.
11. Materu, *Christian Baptism*, 40–50.
12. Sundkler, *A History of the Church*, 548.
13. Materu, *Christian Baptism*, 10–18.

in Africa particularly Tanzania for several centuries."[14] Most of the members of the E.L.C.T Northern Diocese are Chagga people. In the 1960s when the first seven churches merged to form one church, the E.L.C.T, the Northern Diocese was dominated by the Chagga people and the other three major tribes were Pare, Maasai and Meru. As time went on, the number of Christian increased, and people demanded services from the church. These paramount reasons led the Pare in the Eastern part to claim its own diocese, followed by Arusha, and later in 1991 Meru established their own diocese. Therefore, the Northern Diocese as understood in 1963 can be now be traced to the Pare, Arusha and Meru Dioceses, each with one main and dominant ethnic group.

Women and Gender issues in the Chagga Tribe

The Wachagga are a patriarchal ethnic group. According to the Chagga culture, men own and inherit land. Land is regarded as male property inherited patrilineally by males from males or transferred from males to males.[15] Chagga cultures do not allow women to own and inherit land. However, the Chagga women are primary farmers, responsible for tilling the land and growing food crops, but they are rarely credited for these works. In addition, Chagga women take care of coffee plants but do not own coffee plants because of the history of the colonial patriarchy in Kilimanjaro. The colonialists introduced coffee as a cash crop in Chagga land in Kilimanjaro in the early nineteenth century. Eligibility to obtain access to coffee plants depended on ownership of land. Therefore, as Chagga cultures do not allow women to own land, this prevents them from owning coffee plants. Coffee plants are male property. Access to cash crops is thus much more restricted for women than it is for men, even though women do more of the agricultural and domestic labour and bear the fundamental responsibility

---

14. Mwaluko, *Health and Disease*, 1–5.
15. Moore, *Social Facts*, 35–43.

for feeding the household.[16] This historical disadvantage denied women access to cash crops and promoted gender inequalities which promote male-owned material wealth and caused poverty for women.

Furthermore, Chagga women are responsible for feeding domestic animals such as cattle, goat, and sheep. Livestock are fed with fodder from trees, shrubs, banana trees and grass. This is a tedious and heavy workload for women in the Chagga tribe. Domestic animals are reared for milk, for consumption in the home and for sale in local markets. Men are responsible for slaughtering and selling the animals thus controls the monetary gains. Chagga women do not have power to make decisions on the allocation and use of funds from farm products or animal husbandry.

Furthermore, Moore and Puritt point out that in the Chagga tribe the patriarchal customs and practices do not allow the majority of women to be leaders (*Mangi*).[17] Mangi was a title for many male Chagga rulers. The Chaggas have a traditional saying which states: "*Mka chi msongoru-pho, mokaa kanyi na msoro nyi msongoru na mosaura,*" literally means "*women are not rulers; they are custodians of the family and men are rulers and seekers of the needs of families*". This perspective is further discussed in chapter seven in relation to the challenges which deaconess leaders and women leaders face in the Chagga tribe.

Women and Marriage in the Chagga Tribe

In the Chagga tribe, marriage and bearing of the children is respected and considered as a way of continuing life from one generation to another generation. Wachagga believe that God enables husband and wife to start a life.[18] They use a phrase *Ruwa Molunga Soka na Mndo* which means: the being that is capable of joining an axe and sickle. This phrase included God's (*Ruwa's*) mysteri-

---

16. Ibid.
17. Moore, & Puritt, *The Chagga and Meru*, 40–63.
18. Shao, *Bruno Gutman's Missionary Method*, 15–30.

ous powers to see that every living creature found a mate and reproduction was assured. Shao further explains that both axe and sickle are made of metal and have different functions. No one can join them to form a new tool unless they welded. But *Ruwa* can do it without welding them at the same time bring something new out of their union *Ruwa* can do impossible things.[19] He is able to create a new being through intimate relationship between a male and female, as the author of the life. Shao presented a prayer which illustrates how the Chagga people value marriage and childbearing and consider *Ruwa* as the source of all life as well as a good shepherd. This prayer is prayed as follows; "thou God, chief, who pastureth me in trouble like a cow without calf, I pray thee bless me and give me the calf to feel the kraal. I pray thee who are the maker of all things to bless me and give me the child in thy likeness. It is this desire which makes me to stretch out arms towards thee[20]".

Moreover, childbearing increases the respect of a woman in the society. This is also a norm in several tribes in Africa. Thus, Mbiti (1975) argues that bearing of the child in the family is a blessing which assures everyone in the society that woman is able to bear children and her marriage is more secured and relatives respect her and treat her in a good manner.[21] If a person in the Chagga tribe refuses to engage in marriage it means that she/he wants to stop the link between the current generation, ancestors and future generation. In line with this argument, Mbiti claims that failure to get married is like committing a crime against traditional beliefs and practices.[22] This perspective is critically analyzed in chapter seven when discussing the challenges which deaconesses face in the Chagga tribe.

Women's work in the home is not given the same value as that of men outside of the home, therefore, giving the impression that the wife makes no contribution in the acquiring of marital

19. Ibid.
20. Ibid.
21. Mbiti, *Introduction to African Religion*, 104–105.
22. Ibid.

properties. However, traditionally Chagga work has been centred on the farm and is divided by gender. Men's work includes feeding goats, building and maintaining canals, preparing fields, slaughtering animals, and building houses. Women's work includes cutting and collecting firewood and water collection, fodder cutting, cooking, and cleaning the homestead and stalls. Furthermore, women are also in charge of trading in the marketplace. In line with description of women's work, Oduyoye observed: "In assigning roles based on gender, the theory of complementary plays a negative role for women. Patriarchal culture assigns women to perform all domestic duties . . . and allow a man to choose what he wants to be and to do then demands that a woman fills the blanks. Generally, the woman has little or no choice in the matter she has to do."[23] The above quotation portrays the Chagga context where women do not have the opportunity to choose what to do. They perform all activities that men do not want to do in order to sustain their families.

If the husband dies, the wife's marital home is stripped bare by her in-laws who claim the properties left behind as their own.[24] Traditionally, the widow is taken care of by the family of her husband, usually by marrying a brother of her husband, which oppresses women so much. If she refuses to marry her husband's brother, she runs away and finds accommodation somewhere else, and most of them find themselves in the streets with little protection.

Education and Gender among the Chagga

The formal education in the Chagga was introduced by Christian missions. They constructed churches as well as educational institutions and health centres, such as dispensaries. Boys often outnumbered girls in the education facilities because education was not considered important for girls. This can be traced from the

---

23. Oduyeye, *Daughter of Anowa*, 94.
24. Ibid.

time missionaries and colonial governments provided education services in the Chagga tribe and Tanzania at large. Mushi argued that the current inequality of education has been influenced by the missionaries who preferred the education of the boys over and against the girls.[25] This situation was aggravated by the fact that the missionaries who played a role of educating Tanzanians were also converting them to Christianity as a result of their Christian-based school curriculum. The curriculum systematically discriminated against female students by making subject combinations that led to highly-valued and well-paid professions available to boys while denying them to girls. Missionaries minimally educated girls so that they could be good Christian wives of better-educated Christian men and mothers of future Christian children. Also Mushi asserts that the extremely limited employment sector in the colonies did not consider women positively and modern education has imitated that system.[26]

In patriarchal society, some factors are considered to determine whether girls are to be sent to schools or not. According to Stella Bendera in her article titled, "Promoting Education for Girls in Tanzania," she observes that "at household level, cost could be a problem and preference could be given to boys. A girl's labour could be needed more than that of her brother, so that she is kept at home."[27] This shows that girls are more negatively affected by parent's financial inability because girls are more involved in doing farming and domestic activities rather than boys. Also, there are cultural beliefs which limit women to acquire education. For example, Chagga people have a traditional saying which states that *'isomesha mono kyika nyi isomesha mka o mndu'* literary means *'to educate a girl is to educate somebody's wife'*. That means as a girl gets married, her parents will not benefit from her as her income will be channelled to the matters connected to her husband's family. This discourages the patriarchal society to put more efforts to educate girls.

25. Mushi, *History and Development*, 57–60.
26. Ibid.
27. Bendera, *Promoting Education*, 122–25.

Understanding the Context

Moreover, boys can do paying work and earn some money to support their studies, something which is limited to girls. Boys sell firewood, plant trees, keep chickens, and are involved in other trading activities. Thus, they buy their own books and pens to assist their parents by sharing the cost of their education. Girls are involved in household chores and some farm activities, so they do not help their parents much in sharing the cost of their education.[28] Thus, the contribution of girls in Chagga society includes cooking, looking after siblings, fetching water and preparing food, which are very important for production and reproduction within the household. Unfortunately enough, this significant contribution is neither recognized nor rewarded monetarily. This affects their ability to attend schools for financial reasons. When girls are busy at home performing these household tasks, boys are free to play and study. Therefore, the time used by girls for household work seems to be much more valuable than that of boys because their household roles are very important to the well-being of the entire family and must be performed every day. Furthermore, the time used by girls for household tasks increases as they get older. On the other hand, the time used by boys is personal and has limited effect on the family members since they have control over their own time and resources.

Moreover, boys usually study in groups. This helps them to perform well academically compared to the girls who are not allowed by their parents to join group discussion particularly at evening hours. This is because of domestic duties and fear of forming relationships with boys. Also, girls in the Chagga tribe are adversely affected if their father dies. In this situation, some girls withdraw from school in order to take care of other members of the family while their mother engages in income-generating activities to support the family. Chagga experiences show when females are at home, boys do not perform domestic duties at home. They refuse while girls cannot refuse working in the house.

Furthermore, girls from families which depend solely on agriculture drop out during cultivation and harvest. Addition, girls

---

28. Idid.

in the Chagga tribe and all of Tanzania lack helping mechanisms and facilities during the puberty period. As Bendera observes, "Puberty brings new problems for girls for whom there is very few helping mechanism within the school system. There is lack of privacy due to inadequate provision of lavatories."[29] In Chagga and many parts of Tanzania, discussion of puberty is taboo and many girls receive little guidance from either parents or teachers on how to handle the results of their physical while at school. Due to the lack of this knowledge, many girls conceive when they are studying and are expelled from schools. According to Eustella Peter Bhalalusesa, who carried a study on 'Education for All Initiatives and the Barriers to Educating Girls and Young Women in Tanzania,' her study reveals that more than 3,000 primary school girls are expelled annually due to pregnancy.[30] It is very crucial to note that the figure which is mentioned above is likely to be artificially low, because many pregnant girls drop out of schools before the pregnancy start to show in order to avoid the social stigma. Also, adolescents are excluded from contraceptives services in Tanzania. This implies that pregnancy levels among teens in schools are much higher than the available statistics.

Expulsion of the pregnant girls from schools is a violation of the girls' fundamental rights. This contradicts the constitution of Tanzania that gives every citizen the right to education. The constitution of the United Republic of Tanzania of 1977, article XI (2) states: *"Every person has the right to self-education, and every citizen shall be free to pursue education in a field of his choice up to the highest level according to his merits and ability."*

In addition, Tanzania is a signatory to the UN declaration acknowledging that all human beings are equal and deserve the same rights before the law and in the distribution of socio-economic services including education. Furthermore, Tanzania ratified the UN Convention on the Elimination of All Forms of Discrimination against Women (CEDAW) in 1984.

---

29. Ibid.
30. Bhalalusesa, *Education for All Initiatives* 35.

Moreover, Tanzania participated in the World Conference on Women in Beijing in 1995. In addition, Tanzania signed and ratified the international convention on the right to education for girls and women. One would expect Tanzania to be in a very strong position when it comes to promoting the rights of women. However, the above explanations show that this is not the case. Expulsion of girls due to pregnancy is still practiced in Tanzania as explained above. Thus, expulsion of girls due to pregnancy limits the life options for the girl and undermines her potential contribution to the society. In some cases, the fear of expulsion forces the girls to have poor performance and to attempt abortion which is a risk to their lives. On the other hand, pregnancies and health issues particular to women add to day-to-day challenges more for women than men. Furthermore, expelling pregnant schoolgirls seems to punish them for something over which they had little control, as both the girls and boys receive little sex education in Primary and Ordinary secondary school. They have limited access to contraceptive services. There is a need for women's educational empowerment as a way to enable women, particularly girls, to question their rights to education because girls are made to accept the ideology of male supremacy in a patriarchal society. For this matter, women will need powerful social, cultural and economic empowerment to develop a sense of self-worth to pass on to the next generation. Accordingly, since the right to education is just one among many rights that are unknown to the majority of women, there is an urgent need for concerted efforts to provide women's educational empowerment which includes the rights of women.

Conclusion

In this chapter, I have presented an historical overview on the socio-cultural life of the Wachagga and Northern Diocese basin on women and gender issues. The main aim was to explore some gender imbalances which are taking place in the Chagga tribe. It was noted that Chagga cultures do not allow women to own and inherit land. In Chagga tribe marriage and bearing of the children is respected and considered as a way of continuing life from one generation to another generation. If a woman refuses to be married, the members of the society look down upon her. Furthermore, the Chagga cultures do not consider women as leaders but regarded them as custodian of the family. The chapter examined also education and gender issues in the Chagga tribe. It has been observed that there are cultural beliefs which limit women to acquire education. For example, Chagga people have a traditional saying which states 'to educate a girl is to educate somebody's wife'. That means as a girl gets married, her parents will not benefit from her as her income will be channelled to the matters connected to her husband's family. This discourages the patriarchal society to put more efforts to educate girls. In addition, when a female student gets pregnancy is expelled from the school. This expulsion of the pregnant girls from schools affects negatively their future plans to acquire education. The majority of them end up being married at young age because of the cultural influences and pressures from their family members. This chapter also serves as a gateway to the discussion of the Ushirika wa Neema deaconess centre which was established in order to empower women to address their challenges as discussed in the next chapter.

CHAPTER 4

History of *Ushirika wa Neema* Deaconess Ministry

Introduction

USHIRIKA WA NEEMA DEACONESS centre has its roots in the German Protestant tradition of 19th century, and the deaconess movement sprang out of the work of Theodor Fliedner. However, in the New Testament we learn about women who served as deaconesses. One would say that for many years women in the church have been active in performing social and spiritual services and in that way followed the example of Christ. At the same time, this has not necessarily led women into more leadership positions in the church. The patriarchal structure of the church placed women deacons and ministers in a secondary status. It is constructed in a way that men have supreme authority and power in the service.[1]

On the other hand, Fiorenza insists that *diakonia* should challenge those in position of dominance and power to become equal with those who are powerless. Also, she argues that diakonia should create equality from below, not by incorporating those on the bottom of the patriarchal pyramid into its lower ranks. Rather, it should reject the patriarchal hierarchical pyramid. *Diakonia* seeks to level the pyramid by calling those on the top of the pyramid to join the work and labour of those on the bottom and make

1. Fiorenza, *Waiting at Table*, 84–87.

an equal servant class of ministers. This kind of *diakonia* rejects all forms of patriarchal- hierarchical structures and positions and promotes the ministry of equality between women and men.[2] In this chapter, I will present the history of Ushirika wa Neema with reference to the broader history of *diakonia* in the church.

I will begin to examine the origin of deaconess ministry in the New Testament. The focus will on the story of Phoebe who was a woman deacon in the church of Chenchreae. Also, I will discuss how women were included in the ordination of the deaconate ministry and involved in performing ministerial diaconal activities in the church. Thereafter, I will explore the history of deaconess ministry in the Protestant Church. In this respect, I will show how the deaconess ministry started in the nineteenth century in Germany by Kaiserswerth. This foundation will serve to reveal the history of Deaconess at Ushirika wa Neema and the role of the centre in relation to the church and society. The centre performs several diaconic roles in the church and society which are divided into three categories. The first category is charity diakonia. The second category is transformative diakonia which focus on empowering women to improve their situation in the society and church. The last category is stewardship diaconal which focus on stewardship of the earth and the stewardship of the gospel.

Origin of Deaconess Ministry in the New Testament

The name deaconess comes from a Greek word which occurs very frequently in the New Testament. *Diakonia*, as well as its corresponding verb *diakonein*, is used to describe various kinds of services. The other word constantly applied to a servant is *doulos*, which means literally, a slave.[3] The Revised Version Bible distinguishes between these two by rendering *doulos* into English as 'servant' while it translates *diakonos* by the word 'minister.' In

---

2. Ibid, 84–94.
3. Riipinen, *Holy Deaconess*, 1–2.

this case, Riipinen agrees that "*Diakonia* is a Greek word which literally means a servant. This means, providing for physical substance, a servant who is serving food at a family table[4]". According to the Scripture, *diakonia* is one of several gifts of the Holy Spirit (Romans 12:7). This gift enables the church to meet the basic necessities of mankind such as food, clothing, and shelter. Also the apostle Paul in his epistle to Romans shows that the word *diakonos* was used to describe Phoebe as he says: "Phoebe, our sister, who is a servant (diakonos) of the church at Cenchreae. She has often been a helper both to me and many others" (Romans 16:1). Also, in the letter to the Philippians, Paul sends greetings to the bishops and deacons (Philipians1:1). Through the teaching and preaching ministries of the Apostles, the early church grew tremendously with the addition of new believers not only from the native Jewish communities but also from Hellenistic Jews. As the number of the Christians increased, the numbers of needy people increased too. Hellenistic Jews were murmuring because their widows were not attended to effectively. This murmuring was because the Apostles were so occupied by preaching and teaching ministry. They could not leave the ministry of the Word in order to minister at the table. The Apostles saw the need of appointing special people to take charge of the needy people. Hence, they instructed the congregation to appoint seven men (deacons) of good reputations and full of wisdom to take care of the needy people (Acts 6:3). The apostles prayed and laid their hands on newly selected deacons (Acts 6:6).

Thus, Phoebe as a woman deacon in the church of Chenchreae was also included in the ordination of diaconate which called her to perform ministerial diaconal activities in the church. In this case, Offestad shows that Phoebe was a powerful woman with great authority.[5] She was a deaconess who had to take care of the congregation. She was a supporter, provided necessary help which many people needed, protected foreigners and released slaves; she was a mother of the congregation. She also took care of women and sick people. This early ordination of deaconess can also be traced in

4. Ibid, 24.
5. Oftestad, *How to Build a Diaconal Church*, 13.

Empowerment and Autonomy of Women

I Timothy 3:8–12: "Deacons must be men of grave behaviour, they must be examined and if found blameless may afterward serve as deacons. The women must be of grave behaviour, not slanderers, temperate, in every respect faithful. Deacons must be married only once." This passage discusses both male and female deacons. In line with this argument Wijngaards argues:

> The word deacon here is used in its technical sense. It also seems clear that by 'the women' in question who are clearly distinguished from the wives of the deacon while the description of them is parallel to that of the deacon, we must understand women deacons. It indicates a ministry which formed part of the ordained ministry itself. Many scholars agree these women in the ministry are mentioned in the same breath as their male colleagues and seem to be treated as fully equal.[6]

The above quotation proves that in the early church women were ordained as deacons and allowed to perform several duties in the community like men deacons. This claim is also supported by church fathers such as St. Clement of Alexandria and Origen. Here, St. Clement of Alexandria who lived from 150 to 215 said:

> The apostles, giving themselves without respite to the work of evangelism as benefitted their ministry, took with them women, not as wives but as sisters, so that they might serve as their co-ministers, serving women living at home: by their agency the teaching of the Lord reached the women's quarters without arousing suspicion. We are also aware of all the things Paul prescribes on the subject of women deacon in one of the two letters to Timothy.[7]

On the other hand, Origen (c.185—254), a Christian scholar in the Alexandria community, comments on women's diaconate as a valuable institution:

> The text (1Timothy3:11) teaches with the authority of the Apostle that even women are established as deacons

---

6. Wijngaards, *Women Deacons*, 14.
7. Ibid, 15.

in the church. This was the function that was exercised in the community of Cenchreae by Phoebe . . . This pious Phoebe, while offering help and service to all, deserved to assist and serve the Apostle himself. And thus this text teaches at the same time two things: that there are women deacons in the church, and that women, who have given assistance to so many people and who by their good works deserve to be praised by the Apostle, ought to be accepted in the diaconate.[8]

Therefore, the above quotations show that in the second and third centuries, women proceeded to be embedded in diaconal services. This involvement included looking after the physical and material welfare of women, helping orphan children, elderly people, visiting sick people, advising the bishops and priests about the needs of the parishioners.

Furthermore, the Council of Chalcedon (451) discussed the deaconess ministry. It promoted universal ordination of deaconesses. The deaconess ministry was supported by legislation under emperor Justinian 1 of Constantinople (527–65), which attributed an equal legal position to men and women deacons.[9]

In addition with this early history, Deaconesses continue to be recognized and hold office within parts of the Lutheran Church. However, Lutherans do not have a standardized formal training program which is the same everywhere. In the Lutheran Church, deaconesses are allowed to marry while in some places like ELCT-Northern Diocese, deaconesses voluntarily live the celibate life. The Lutheran Church does not force deaconesses to enter the vow of celibacy. Also it does not force deaconesses to stay in celibacy if she feels not to have a call of living an unmarried life. They have a freedom to leave the celibate life and marry. The following section explains the history of deaconess ministry in the protestant church.

---

8. Ibid.
9. Ibid, 10–25.

History of Deaconess Ministry in the Protestant Church

In the protestant church, the deaconess ministry that started in the nineteenth century originated in Kaiserswerth in Germany. As Nordstokke[10] argues, Theodor Fliedner (1800–1864) was among the first German pastors in Kaiserswerth who in 1836 opened the hospital and deaconesses training centre, which provided diaconal services to the needy people in the community. According to the letter from Sr. Dietlinde, Hofmann[11] claims that the Napoleonic wars[12] created impoverished conditions for many people in Germany. The most affected victims were widows, orphans and elderly people who could not adequately be cared for by inadequate government relief. Furthermore, the end of the wars also marked the beginning of industrialization and mechanization. This era adversely impacted on many people, who had been depending on the traditional economy, including single women of higher social classes, who were displaced and forced to find other ways of supporting themselves. Some researchers have reported that industrialization and significant population growth also brought with them urbanization and congested cities and the people who flocked to the cities in the first half of the nineteenth century encountered several problems like diseases such as cholera. Hospitals were very few and not be able to help all victims. This situation forced the pa-

---

10. Nordstokke, *Liberating Diakonia*, 30.

11. See Appendix 5: The Testimony of the First Missionaries at Ushirika wa Neema (Sr. Dietlinde Hofmann and Sr. Gisela).

12. The Napoleonic Wars were a series of conflicts fought between France under the leadership of Napoleon Bonaparte and a number of European nations between 1799 and 1815. They followed on from the War of the First Coalition (1793–97) and engaged nearly all European nations in a bloody struggle, a struggle that also spilled over into Egypt, America and South America. The first campaign of the Napoleonic wars was the War of the second Coalition. With Bonaparte absent in Egypt fighting the British, a new coalition formed against the French in 1798. This consisted of Russia, Great Britain, Austria, Portugal, the Ottoman Empire and the Kingdom of Naples. Retrieved from: http://www.historyofwar.org/articles/wars_napoleonic.html.

tients to be responsible for their own care in some cases; they were assisted by poorly trained servants.[13] This situation promoted the leaders of rival movements in Germany to combine social action and evangelism in order to improve these harsh conditions. This approach addressed both spiritual and physical needs.

Fliedner, a Lutheran pastor, in 1822 was assigned to a union parish, that is, a combination of a Lutheran and reformed parish in the predominantly Catholic town of Kaiserwerth. His parish faced a financial crisis. To rescue the situation, he decided to make a trip in 1823 and 1824 to the Netherlands and learned how urban Christian charity was practiced in several hospitals, orphanages and elderly homes. He adopted these practices to eliminate vulnerable conditions which affected many people in Germany.[14]

In 1833, Pastor Fliedner and his first wife, Friederike, established an asylum for released female prisoners. Also they opened a sewing school for poor children in 1835, and in 1836 Pastor Fliedner opened a deaconess institution at Kaiserwerth.[15] The main role of this deaconess institution was to train women to participate in various types of social work, particularly nursing and teaching. The field of diaconal work expanded in the second half of the 19th century and included orphanages, asylums mental hospitals and poorhouses.[16] During that era Kaiserwerth become a model of diaconal work in Germany and the entirety of Europe as well as America.

Ushirika wa Neema adopted the deaconess motherhouse organizational model found in Augsburg, Kaiserwerth and Strasburg. In this system, deaconesses relate to one another as sisters and live in a motherhouse since 1980. They live as children to parents. Sr Agness Lema is a mother of deaconesses at *Ushirika wa Neema* and Rev Aron Urioh is chaplain and considered as a father of deaconesses. In the same way Rector Steghofer and Sr. Lise Lote were viewed as surrogate parents at the Augsburg motherhouse.

13. Green, *Responding to Secularization*, 17.
14. Ibid.
15. Ibid.
16. Nordstokke, *Liberating Diakonia*, 30–39.

EMPOWERMENT AND AUTONOMY OF WOMEN

History of Deaconess at Ushirika wa Neema in the Northern Diocese

This presentation of the history is very much based on oral sources and communications I have had with significant people in the Northern Diocese and Mother House in Augsburg, Germany. The history of the deaconess centre is not written, so the following represents a first attempt to collect important parts of this history and present them. In my presentation, I am especially concerned with elements that highlight this thesis' problem statement regarding the empowerment of women. While there were different motivations behind the establishment of Ushirika wa Neema deaconess centre, in this study, the priority is on feminist motives; others were social and economical.

Emancipation of Women

According to the Mother of deaconesses, Ushirika wa Neema Deaconess Centre was established in order to support and promote the ministry of women in the diocese, which means the issue of empowerment of women was part of the motivation behind. It created a space which provides a tool to address some female issues. The centre recognized that some women had special problems which were difficult to be attended to by male pastors. In that time, the Diocese had not allowed the ordination of women because of the oppressive patriarchal cultures which subordinated women. Therefore, some females started to demand a place where they could get counselling for their private matters. It was difficult for women in the church to share some of their personal problems with male pastors. Some of their problems were private. They didn't like men to know them. This agrees with Hugh, who argues that in the Eastern Church the office of "deaconess" was established in order to address women issues in the church. As she states:

> Those that please thee out of all the people thou shall choose and appoint as deacons: a man for the performance of the most things that are required, **but a woman**

History of Ushirika wa Neema Deaconess Ministry

> for the ministry of women . . . office of a woman deacon is required . . . For our Lord and Saviour also was ministered unto by women ministers, Mary Magdalene, and Mary the daughter of James and mother of Joseph, and the mother of the sons of Zebedee, with other women beside. And thou also hast need of the ministry of a deaconess for many things; for a deaconess is required to visit those who are sick, and to minister to them in that of which they have need, and to bathe those who have begun to recover from sickness.[17]

In this case, Hugh mentioned some importance of having deaconesses in the church. Among them is to minister women's needs and bathe those who are sick, something which is difficult to be done by male ministers.

In the Diocese during the 1960s there was the emancipation of women and girls who wanted to be free from patriarchal cultures.[18] They wanted to exercise their independent freedom which is free from marriage and family burdens in order to serve Christ. At that time, women were considered as the mother of households. They were custodians of the family while men were considered as rational whose work was in the public sphere. They wanted to cross this border of women's oppression. They had an intrinsic motivation to serve the Lord as deaconess sisters and help their fellow women to improve their lives.

The Mother of deaconesses claims that Ushirika wa Neema was established in order to provide a place where women and girls who decided to live the communal and celibate life could have the freedom to do that. A special place was needed because in the Chagga tribe, marriage is regarded as a norm. Women who choose to remain single are usually stigmatized and forced by the society to marry. To minimize the stigma, Ushirika wa Neema become a centre where women and girls who decided to serve Christ by living a celibate life are given love and skills which make them independent.

17. Hugh, *Didascalia Apostolorum*, 18.

18. Interview with Rev. Aaron Urio (Chaplain of UWN) on 16.07.2012. Moshi.

Empowerment and Autonomy of Women

Furthermore, according to Erasto Kweka, the former Bishop of the Northern Diocese, in the 1960s a group of girls from Christian Fellowship Organizations in secondary schools in the Kilimanjaro region went to the diocese leaders and expressed their passion to serve the church and community as deaconess sisters.[19] They seemed to be inspired by Roman Catholic sisters because they posed a critical question to church leaders: Why does the ELCT-Northern Diocese not have a deaconess sisterhood like Roman Catholics? At that time this idea of deaconess sisterhood was not accepted by the diocese executive committee. Instead they were encouraged to be parish workers and Sunday school teachers. However, in the 1970s these female students returned with the same request to Bishop Kweka. He was impressed with their willingness to live a celibate life and serve Christ in the church and community. He shared this idea with Shedrack Ngowi who was the general secretary of the ELCT-Northern Diocese. He supported the bishop's view about a deaconess centre and they both convinced the executive committee to accept the request of these girls. This time the executive committee accepted it.

Social Motivation

Bishop Kweka said that in 1970s there was a decline in the number of the church institutions such as hospitals. He noted that the Roman Catholics were doing very well because some of their institutions were supervised by nuns. This motivated him to foster the establishment of the centre in order to prepare faithful and committed women and girls who would serve in church institutions and the church in general. The motivation was to recruit and promote trusted servants of God who could serve as Sunday school teachers, and social workers in the church institutions. In line with this argument, the Mother of deaconesses asserts that the purpose of establishing Ushirika wa Neema was to prepare deaconesses so that they could provide diaconal services to marginalized and

---

19. Interview with Retired Bishop Dr. Erasto N. Kweka on 03.07.2012. Moshi.

needy people in the church and community. The focus was to prepare them to provide services in the hospitals, centers for disabled people, orphans, elderly and sick people who are helpless.

Moral and Ethical Motivations

Aaron Urioh, who is Chaplain at Ushirika wa Neema, pointed out that another motivation to establish Ushirika wa Neema was to prepare deaconesses in order they might provide social and ethical services in learning institutions. He said: "Learning institutions and vocational training centres needed leaders and workers who have good Christian faith backgrounds, who are faithful and committed to fulfil their responsibilities and to be a light and good salt in the community."[20] These words indicate that there was a moral motivation of establishing the Deaconess Centre of Ushirika wa Neema in order to get faithful workers in learning institutions who could be a model and example to follow. This perhaps could contribute to mould the learners in those institutions to be good citizens. Aaron Urioh makes it clear by saying: Some of deaconesses are matrons and discipline leaders in different schools and vocation training centers of our diocese.[21] Therefore, the above discussion indicates that emancipation of women, social factors, moral and ethical motivations were internal motives which led to the establishment of Ushirika wa Neema deaconess centre. After examining the internal motives, in the following paragraph I will examine external motive for establishment of Ushirika wa Neema.

---

20. Interview with Rev. Aaron Urio (Chaplain of UWN) on 16.07.2012, Moshi.

21. Interview with Rev. Aaron Urio (Chaplain of UWN) on 16.07.2012, Moshi.

German Contributions in the Establishment of Ushirika wa Neema

The Ushirika wa Neema Deaconess Centre was established because it received moral and material assistance from the Mother House in Augsburg, Germany. In 1979, the Mother House in Augsburg, Germany, sent two deaconesses, Gisela and Dietlinde, to the Northern Diocese to establish the Ushirika wa Neema Deaconess Centre. Furthermore, the Mother House in Augsburg financed the construction of this centre and sent two architects who supervised its construction.

Organization of Ushirika was Neema Diaconess Centre

Leadership and Organization

Ushirika wa Neema has a board of directors chaired by the Bishop of the ELCT Northern Diocese. The board has 19 members appointed by the ELCT Northern Diocese Council. Among them nine are women and ten are men. Ushirika wa Neema has five representatives on the board. Deaconesses are led by the Mother of the deaconess house and two chaplains. The centre has an internal administrative structure which is chaired by the Mother of the deaconess house. Its members involve the directors of different sectors which are under the centre.

Devotional Life

At the Deaconess Centre of Ushirika wa Neema, devotional life is considered as a part and parcel of every one's life. The deaconesses have daily devotional services; they conduct Bible studies, retreats, and fellowships. They make sure that its community and other people in the society are fully involved in knowing and witnessing Jesus Christ. They have a responsibility of praying every day. They have morning prayers, afternoon prayers and evening prayers. They live the life that portrays their calling.

Qualification of Deaconesses

The following requirements were mentioned by the Mother of deaconesses as qualifications to become a deaconess at Ushirika wa Neema:

- Inner calling
- Acceptance and confirmation by parish (recommendation letter from parish is compulsory)
- Age should be between 20–30
- Ability to make decisions
- Permission from parents
- Must be standard seven leaver and above
- Good health

Ushirika wa Neema enrols girls from different denominations without discrimination. Rev. Mlaki who is assistant chaplain argues that Sisters who join the convent from other denominations do so out of their own desire and interest in Lutheran dogma and doctrine, so they may slightly be called converts.[22] At the convent they get a series of teachings in the Lutheran heritage so in this way they continue growing in Lutheranism.

Consecration of Sisters

A sister will officially be consecrated to a lifelong sisterhood out of her own will after staying in the convent for nine (9) years as a probationary sister. The consecration is normally done by the presiding bishop of the diocese at the cathedral. During the consecration

---

22. Interview with Rev. Daniel Mlaki (Assistant Chaplain of UWN) on 27.07.2012. Moshi.

ceremony in the liturgy, every lifelong sister will be given a ring as a sign of commitment and faithfulness to the call and service, as well as a cross as a sign of sharing Christ's victory and suffering in her life as a servant.

[B] Deaconess Regulations

The mother of deaconesses at Ushirika wa Neema identified several rules which govern the behaviour of all deaconesses at Ushirika wa Neema. The aim of this rule is to strengthen and reinforce a deaconess's connection to her surrogate family. The first rule is that deaconesses at Ushirika wa Neema have to live celibate life. This agrees with Green who argues that "to enter the institution's service, a woman could not be bound to marriage or to service in some other way and this was because a deaconess must be free from such connection in order that her work may not be hindered."[23] The argument here is that a woman who is a wife or a mother cannot devote herself full time to help the poor and work as deaconess. To be wife or mother means that one is required to perform some responsibilities which are connected to these roles within her own household. Green says, the reason for prohibiting marriage for deaconesses was not rooted in the ideas that celibacy was a higher spiritual calling, but in the belief that a women could not serve two households.[24] A woman's calling was to serve the one household to which she belonged. A deaconess has to commit herself to the spiritual household of the motherhouse and to carry out the responsibilities and duties associated with it. If she decides to marry, she is compelled to leave the motherhouse so that she can devote all of her energy to fulfil the responsibilities of her new household.

Furthermore, deaconess at Ushirika wa Neema are required to be obedient to their leaders. The Mother of the deaconesses said that "our deaconess sisters are required to respect their leaders and

---

23. Green, *Responding to Secularization,* 60.
24. Ibid, 61.

each human being. This creates an environment that is conducive to fostering our communal life."

Deaconesses at Ushirika wa Neema are not dependent upon presents from their clients when they are doing diaconal services. They rely on the Ushirika wa Neema Deaconess Centre to give them their basic needs including food, clothes and shelter. Some of the sisters are working outside of Ushirika wa Neema; therefore, the leaders of the motherhouse negotiate with the leaders of the institutions where the sisters work to ensure that sisters get their basic needs. The deaconess is not required to find support herself independently by doing extra work in order to receive extra payment. Ushirika wa Neema provides all basic needs for deaconesses.

The mother system of Ushirika wa Neema has special uniforms for deaconesses. Ushirika wa Neema introduced the common uniform at the first consecration in 1989. Mother of deaconess insists, "Our uniform is a symbol of equality which also means that among us no one is more privileged than another, regardless of her social class background." There is a perception that this uniform is used to identify the deaconesses in the public sphere and contribute to some extent to prevent men who might attempt to make sexual advances upon them. Also the dressing of this uniform promotes deaconesses status and respect in the society and church.

The motherhouse system at Ushirika wa Neema provides deaconesses in many respects with a surrogate family, a spiritual household. In this motherhouse, they are cared for and given basic needs. They are educated and trained for several works in this household. They support one another in their task as a family member. A deaconess belongs to the motherhouse at Ushirika wa Neema wherever she works; she does so as a member and representative of Ushirika wa Neema. Deaconesses are also ensured a place of burial. They have a special plot in their compound for burying deaconesses. This implies that deaconesses belong to Ushirika wa Neema for their whole lives.

Empowerment and Autonomy of Women

Role of Ushirika wa Neema Deaconess Centre

This subsection explores the diaconic role of Ushirika wa Neema (UwN) deaconess centre in the ELCT-ND. The centre performs several diaconic roles in the church and society which are divided into three categories. The first category is charity diakonia. UwN provides charity diaconal services to orphans, sick, aged people and the needy people. They own one orphanage centre and one college for training caretakers. The second category is transformative diakonia which focus on empowering women to improve their situation in the society and church. The centre prepares deaconesses who go into parishes to train women important skills for life, such as gardening, keeping animals and catering. The centre also owns the Montessori Kindergarten College which is used to train kindergarten teachers. The centre is running different projects such as soap making, Christian book shops, wafer making, importing wine from Spain and supplying it to different parishes of the ELCT–ND and other dioceses. The last category is stewardship diakonia.

Charitable Diakonia

According to Riipinen, charity diakonia "is an expression of Christian love, which the church is called to practice."[25] This approach involves providing food for the hungry and helping marginalized people such as orphans, sick, and disabled people. Charitable diakonia makes God's presence and the church to be visible in the world. As Rev Aaron Urioh a chaplain at Ushirika wa Neema argues in his article known as *"Kanisa bila udiakonia halina uhai"* literally translated *"The church is not alive without diaconical ministry"*, charitable diakonia is the identity of the church to the society. Diaconical ministry helps the society to recognize the importance of the church and also it witnesses the Jesus' work in the church.

Moreover, LWF states "As Lutheran churches we base our faith understanding of diaconical ministry on the scriptures. The

---

25. Riipinen, *Holy Deaconess*, 23.

ultimate point of reference is Jesus Christ himself. The canon of the diaconal ministry is Jesus self designation as a "deacon" "forever the son of man did not come to be served but to serve, and to give his life a ramson for many" (Mark 10:45). Charitable diakonia embody God's love for the world acted out through Jesus' life, witness, death and resurrection. Furthermore, Jesus preached the good News of God's kingdom on earth that sought to give the world in its abundance (John 10:10). Jesus did that in several ways such as; preaching and teaching God's grace to sick and calling them to repent their sins. He also healed the sick people and cast out demons and evil forces that inflicted suffering on human beings. He reached out and integrated with people who were neglected marginalized and excluded in the society. By doing so, Jesus shaped and laid foundation of diaconal ministry in his ministry. The diaconal ministry shows the present of Jesus among the needy and those who struggle for dignity and survival like orphans.

Diaconic Ministry to Orphans

The centre provides diaconal services to orphans. An orphan means a child whose parents have died. Orphan comes from Greek word "*orphanos*" which means a person who has been deprived through death of both parents. However, the word orphan is also used for someone who has lost one parent.[26] There are different types of orphans. Those who are maternal orphans—these are children under age of 18 years whose mother has died. Parental orphans—these, are children under age of 18 years whose father has died. Total orphans—these are children under age of 18 both of whose parents have died. These children need to be brought up by given essential basic needs such as food, shelter, and clothing to enable them to cope with other children in the society. The main cause of orphanhood is death. Death causes orphanhood because it takes away a person's parent or parents. Parents may die due to sickness or accidents. However, since the outbreak of HIV, there

---

26. New Dictionary of Christian Ethics, *Orphan*, 223.

is an increase of death cases and it causes the increasing number of orphans. According to the Joint United Nations Program on HIV/AIDS (UNAID); Tanzania had 1.3 million adults and children living with HIV/AIDS, with 1,100,000 children orphaned by HIV/AIDS in 2000. In 2002, the national adult HIV prevalence was 7.8%, with children living with HIV/AIDS at 30% who got it during pregnancy, delivery and 10% though breast feeding.[27] HIV/AIDS kill parents and increasing the number of orphans, widow, widowers, further, production decreases because of losing manpower. Elderly people are suffering as they lose their children and some left with orphans who depend on them. This brings a challenge to the church on how to serve people who need both spiritual and physical help. Mmbando et al reported that in Tanzania there were 1 million children without parents due to HIV/AIDS. Among that number 40,000 are infected with HIV. Even though there are NGOs and community based organization to help these children, still many orphans are not attended.[28]

There are several problems facing orphans in the society. Some of the orphans practice immoralities such as prostitution, robbery, theft, drug abuse, murder and some become street children, not because they like it but because of economic problems. Several studies have reported that many orphans lack enough basic needs. For example a study carried by Pastor David Lyamuya presented a case of how orphans face some challenges in their lives. One case is presented below: "Elisa Mariki of 13 years old says: I am sad and lonely because I used to live with my beloved parents and then all of a sudden they are all gone forever. I am real missing them. Our grandparents are very old, sick and weak, they cannot provide us with our needs and that is why my brother have left home and turned up being a street boy. I am afraid that they will kill him."[29] According to above excerpt, some of the orphans suffer a lot and decided to become street children and find simple

---

27. WCC: The Church Confronted with the Problem of HIV/AIDS.
28. Mmbando et al, *Care for the most vulnerable,* 13–21.
29. Lyamuya, *The Ministry of the Church,* 25.

jobs so as to get their needs. As a result they become slaves of the society without any appropriate.

The centre seeks to provide diaconical services to the marginalized people such as orphans and street children. Rev. Urioh a Chaplain at UwN said:

> We provide diakonia services to the marginalized groups in the church and society in order to restore and transform their lives. We have established an orphanage centre at Kalali which take care of orphans from age of one day and above. Deaconesses at UwN also tend to visit and provide diaconal services to the street children at Kili centre and Amani centre in Moshi town. They provide them food, clothes and the word of God. This diaconal service makes the church to be alive in people's lives and become an identity of the church in the society.

Therefore, diaconal praxis always takes place in real life where people suffer, experience poverty, violence and injustice or whatever might threaten their dignity as human beings.[30] This implies that the deaconesses at UwN reach need people through diaconal ministry which makes the gospel practical in their lives. The church has the responsibility of taking care of man's life holistically—spiritually, physically, and mentally. This make diaconal ministry very essential ministry in the church, such as when Nordstokke states that: "Diakonia is central to what it means to be the church. As a core component of the gospel, diakonia is not option but an essential part of discipleship. Diakonia reaches out to all persons, who are created in God's image. While diakonia begins as unconditional services to the neighbour in need, it leads inevitably to social change that restores, reforms and transforms."[31]

The above quotation implies that diaconal services to marginalized people enable them to see the love of Christ and fosters changes in their lives. Even the Bible insists that orphans and widows should be protected and that their advantages should not be taken away from them. For example Exodus 22: 22–24 "do not

---

30. Nordstokke, *Liberating Diakonia,* 10–15.
31. Ibid, 13.

take advantage of a widow or an orphan. If you do and they cry out to me, I will certainly hear their cry. My anger will be aroused, and I will kill you with the sword; your wives will become widows and your children fatherless." There is a need to protect the orphans and widows. This is crucial due to the fact that these are two groups of people who are at high risk of losing their inheritance rights of the property of their parents or husbands if they are not well protected.

Deaconic Ministry to Disabled People

Deaconesses at Ushirika wa Neema provide diaconal services to disabled people such as handicapped children and elderly people in the church and society. They are working with other centers which provide social services and training on different skills to the disabled. Thus, the skills the handicapped children get increase their self-esteem and give them a feeling of being able to contribute to the community. It empowers the children to integrate with other people in their community.

Deaconesses provide other diaconal services to the marginalize people in the society. Due to the increase of needy people in the society, UwN decided to establish a college for training home care givers who provide diaconal services to elderly and disabled people. Furthermore, Green argues that deaconesses are called to serve the poor, the sick, the prisoners, children and others in need in the same way as the Lord served such people in his era. He further claimed that as the Lord showed the compassion to these people in order to save them from their sins and offer them forgiveness in the same vein, a deaconess has to perform acts of love to open their hearts to the world and ultimately to give them an opportunity to find forgiveness and salvation with the Lord.[32]

Moreover, Green points out that deaconess are called to help people who are in need, they should bring God's kingdom close to people by addressing the physical needs of their fellow human.

---

32. Green, *Responding to Secularization*, 54.

History of *Ushirika wa Neema* Deaconess Ministry

Deaconesses also address the spiritual needs of the people. This work of love is a useful way of promoting evangelism. Deaconesses dedicated their energy and life to caring for those who in need because this is the particular calling God had given them.

The almighty God is present in the world as creator, savior, and the life giver. Diaconal ministry makes God's presence and the church visible in the world. As Urioh[33] argues, the diaconal ministry is the identity which enables society to recognize the importance of the church and also witness Jesus' work through the church.

Therefore, deaconesses at UwN devote their life to care for poor, sick, disabled and assisting pastors during the services, teaching kindergartens, teaching Christian education in primary and secondary schools, as well as providing counselling to students in both primary and secondary schools. In the same vein, Groh, who explored the role of deaconess through the ages with the focus on Lutheran deaconess association, argued that the role of deaconesses includes: administering to the poor and sick, doing parish work and teaching, helping the sick and needy, comforting the distressed and suffering such as the martyrs.[34] She further claimed that deaconesses are responsible for instructing catechumens and assist the pastor during the baptism of women. This view agrees with Ruth W. Rasche who researched on 'the Deaconess Sisters: Pioneer Professional Women' in St. Louis-Evangelical. The author argued that the role of deaconesses is to nurse the sick and take care for the poor and aged.[35] So, deaconesses, just like Jesus, help their fellow human beings from the cradle to the grave. On the other hand, deaconesses provide transformative diakonia in the church and society as well.

---

33. Urio, *Kanisa na Huduma,* 20.
34. Groh, *The Role of Deaconess,* 19.
35. Rasche, *The Deaconess Sisters,* 94–109.

Transformative Diakonia

Transformative diakonia is a continuous process of rejection of issues which dehumanize and violate life and of adherence to what affirms the sanctity of life and gifts bestowed in everyone, thus promoting peace and justice in society.[36] Riipinen[37] argues that transformative diakonia liberates people from ignorance and opens their eyes to the realities of their situation. It helps them to see why they are poor and how to overcome it. It promotes improvement and positive changes in the function and appearance of social life, culture, economy and politics. Transformative diakonia involves the achievement of certain goals, of arriving at a new situation where human dignity is more respected with peace and justice for more people. Thus, transformation is closely related to what also may be called as social change, progress, development and empowerment. UwN Deaconess Centre seems to contribute to the transformative diakonia through fostering female education and economy which seeks to improve women's status and situation in the church and society. This will be discussed in detail in later chapters.

Stewardship Diakonia

Ushirika wa Neema emphasis the role of stewardship. This key word can literally mean the way in which someone controls and looks after an event or organization. Furthermore, some scholars discussed the concept of stewardship in the light of grace, that is, "everything comes from God as a gift and is to be administered faithfully on his behalf."[38] It further indicates that there are two kinds of stewardship. The first one is stewardship of the earth and the second one is the stewardship of the gospel.[39] Ushirika wa Neema put emphasis on both aspects of stewardship, that is,

---

36. Nordstokke, *Empowerment*, 185 -195.
37. Riipinen, *Holy Deaconess*, 34.
38. New Dictionary of Theology *Stewardship*, 123.
39. Ibid.

they are keen about making sure that the earth is well kept and at the same time the word of God is properly administered. Paying attention on the stewardship of the earth, the main issue to consider is how serious one is, about the earth on which she/he is living. This is well measured on how one is serious about keeping God's creation. In illuminating how UwN practices this role, they are keen about stewardship of the earthy. One deaconess said: "We are trying at our level best to conserve the environment. For instance, we are cooking by using biogas which produced from organic waste particularly from our cow and pigs' waste. Women from different parishes tend to visit our centre in order to learn how to make and use biogas from animals' waste."

The above excerpt shows that deaconess sisters use animal waste products to produce gas which is useful for cooking. The Majority of populations in Tanzania and other developing countries still depend on traditional wood fuels for their energy needs which contributes to deforestation and desertification.[40] Thus domestic biogas at UwN promotes the stewardship of the earth as it focuses on environmental conservation because it reduces the high consumption of wood fuel which contributes to deforestation and soil degradation. This resulted to the reduction of Global Greenhouse Gas (GHG) emissions results in a significant scientific attention at present.[41] It has been stated that the burning of fossil fuels and deforestation by burning are the most significant human contributions causing increases in the main GHG, carbon dioxide (CO_2).[42] Biogas production is reported to be among the measures to reduce methane emissions from wastes.[43] It considered as a most appropriate mitigation strategy to reduce atmospheric methane emissions which destroy the ozone layer and contribute to the global warming. In a nutshell, biogas project at UwN fosters stewardship of the earth through:

---

40. Barry et al, *Selection of renewable energy*, 45–52.
41. Parmesan, and Gary, *A globally coherent fingerprint*, 37–42.
42. McGregor, *Global Greenhouse Gas*, 285.
43. Friedrich, *Quantification of greenhouse*, 1585–1596.

- Protecting forests
- Reducing the emission of toxic gases which affect the ozone layer
- Improving hygienic conditions
- Producing Electricity
- Improving the rural standard of living

Moreover, UwN promote the stewardship of the earth though planting trees in their compounds. One deaconess said: "We are keeping our compound beautiful through planting trees, green plants, floors, fruit trees and cultivating our farms by using environmental friendly methods such as crop rotation, terraces, contour and manure."

According to the above informant, it seems as if Ushirika wa Neema uses friendly farming methods which are very vital for improving soil structure and protecting the soil against erosion and nutrient losses. Furthermore, the informant points out that Ushirika wa Neema plays a key role of conserving the environment by planting trees which is very important for reducing global warming and providing shade as well as beautiful landscape in their compound.

These trees play an important role of renewing the atmosphere. This is due to the fact that plants, particularly green plants, produce oxygen. Not only that but also they remove carbon dioxide from the air which contributes to distorting earth's climate. All living organisms need oxygen. If green plants do not supply oxygen, life would stop. Also, the use of manure, terraces, and crop rotation is very vital for conserving the environment against soil erosion and degradation.

Furthermore, UwN deals with the well being of the society in making sure that people live a pleasant life. UwN has spread its ministry in many parts of the Northern diocese. Among the tasks they do which symbolize their keenness in stewardship of the earth are mentioned by Mother of the deaconesses as explained below: "We are preparing faithful servants who serve as social workers, nurses, agricultural specialists, and caretakers who provide care to the orphans and disabilities". All these roles portray stewardship which in one way or another sustains God's creation here on the earth.

In the same vein, Nkya reports: "UwN is participating in the stewardship of the earth by keeping the sustainability of the creation for future generation, especially the children, animals, plants and water. The good use of resources and project available for future generation that finds life sustainable on the earth is what is reckoned as stewardship."[44] The above quotation implies that Deaconesses Sisters at UwN stand for the service of the God and fellow human being, seeking the will of God and a better life for their fellow human beings.

Conclusion

This fourth chapter has presented the origin and formation of Ushirika wa Neema deaconess ministry in ELCT-Northern Diocese. In analyzing the history of deaconess sisters I discussed how women were included in the ordination of deaconate ministry and involved in performing ministerial diaconal activities in the church. Thereafter, I explored the history of deaconess ministry in the Protestant Church. In this respect, I showed how the deaconess ministry started in the nineteenth century in Germany by Kaiserswerth. Moreover, I examined history of Deaconess at Ushirika wa Neema and the role of the centre to the church and society in performing various diaconal roles. The centre performs several diaconic roles in the church and society which are divided into three categories namely, charity diakonia, transformative diakonia and stewardship diaconal. The next chapter examines the third wave feminist theories because it involves economic, political, social, and personal empowerment of women. Also, it focuses more on the individual empowerment of women rather than on activism.

---

44. Nkya, *The role of Ushrika wa Neema*, (2008).

CHAPTER 5

Third-Wave Feminism and Empowerment Theories

___

Introduction

This chapter discusses the Third-Wave feminism theories which began in the 1990s to the present. These theories are crucial because they involve the economic, political, social, and personal empowerment of women. However, this chapter is divided into several sub-sections which are: The Third-Wave of Feminism Theories, Empowerment Approach, Origin of the Empowerment, Empowerment Views and Power as a Process of Human Relations, Components of Women Empowerment, Women Empowerment, Economic Empowerment and Educational Empowerment.

Third-Wave Feminist Theories

Third-Wave feminism is a feminist movement that began in the 1990s. It involves economic, political, social, and personal empowerment of women. Also, it focuses more on the individual empowerment of women than on activism. It promotes women to build meaningful identities in the complex contemporary world. Third-Wave feminism encourages personal empowerment and action as a starting point for promoting changes in the society. It involves diversity of women compared to the second-wave feminism which

Third-Wave Feminism and Empowerment Theories

focused on middle-class white women. It usually includes antiracism, postcolonial theories, postmodernism theories, broader construction of gender, and subordination of women and how to empower them in different contexts.[1]

The rise of feminist theories has been a special approach which empowers women to challenge gender inequalities in the society with the focus of promoting positive changes. Feminist researchers have conducted several studies which identify gender inequalities in the society and church. For instance, young insists that women should identify their oppressions which are around them and find ways to get rid of them. She further argues:

> *Feminist theology draws on the broader project of feminist theory. Although feminists differ in the ways they analyze women's oppression, they do agree on certain fundamental themes. Arising out of feminist consciousness and feminist political and social action, feminist theory recognizes the systematic oppression of women and encourages women to name their oppression and to ponder its sources. Various feminist theorists see the importance of providing a theoretical accounting of women's situation so as to understand the communality of women's oppression on the one hand while not denying variety of women's experiences on the other.*[2]

The above quote indicates that women oppression is not homogeneous in the universal. They differ from one context to another. Feminist theorists agree that it is very important to explore the experience of women in each context by making women a centre of focus and finding ways to liberate them from gender inequality which favours men. Similarly, Oduyoye and King argue that women empowerment involves understanding and awareness of subordination around women and finding appropriate ways to eliminate it. By doing so, women gain power to promote positive changes in the church and society which improve their situations. For this to happen, supportive environments should be provided,

1. Mason, *Feminist Waves*, 23.
2. Young, *Throwing like a girl*, 11–12.

for instance, women seminars, amendment of oppressive laws, and gender education.[3] This is discussed in details in chapter six on how Ushirika wa Neema conducted women seminars which helped widows and women in general to be aware of patriarchal practices like customary laws which oppress them and how to address their needs like inheritance of property through amended laws.

Moreover, Oduyoye and Kanyoro explored women experiences in society and church. Their research revealed that African culture and Bible tradition are patriarchal and been used to dominate women. Although these are culture forms identity for people, African women theologians stated that not everything in culture supports the well being of women. Therefore, women should be empowered to advocate for the change in societies. UWN promote women's rights and empowerment and insists that women are people like men and they should be treated equally. This perspective is used in chapter six to discuss Chagga patriarchal culture which rejects women leadership. Oduyoye insists that women's empowerment promotes the partnership and solidarity of men and women in the church and society.[4]

According to Oduyoye, such solidarity implies that churches are called to work hand in hand with women to ensure that the rights and needs of women are highlighted. Oduyoye insists that the church is made up of both men and women; thus, the church should recognize that women can contribute positive things in the church and society as men do. Therefore, men and women need to learn and appreciate the role played by each other in order to bring a full communion within the body of Christ.[5] Furthermore, Oduyoye points out women cannot tackle gender injustices themselves; they need the assistance of men. Her argument is that both men and women should participate and co-operate together so that the church can be a place where both men and women serve the Lord with equal respect and mutual understanding. Oduyoye caution

3. Ezer, *Inheritance Law*, 35.
4. Oduyoye, *Who Will Roll the Stone Away?*, 45–50.
5. Ibid, 49.

that this should be done in a way which does not let women be assimilated into existing structures of dominance, patriarchy and hierarchy in the church and society. She further insists that for this collaboration of women and men to be sustainable in the church there should be establishment of partnerships and the sharing of ecclesial responsibilities.[6] However, the main question here is: how should partnerships between men and women be accomplished in the church? In this case, Oduyoye comments that the church should promote equity in representation within the various church bodies. Also the church should encourage participation of women in decision making. This calls for empowerment of women to be given priority in the church and society.

Empowerment Approach

The word empowerment can be used in many ways and in wide range of contexts. Therefore, empowerment can be defined as the process by which people become aware of their own interests and those related to the interests of others, in order both to participate from a position of greater strength in decision-making and actually to influence such decisions.[7] Moreover, empowerment is the process by which the powerless gain greater control over the circumstances of their lives. It includes both control over resources (physical, human, intellectual, financial) and over ideology (beliefs, values and attitudes) Vayrynen.[8] Furthermore, UNESCO states: "Empowerment is about people, both women and men, taking control over their lives: setting their own agendas, developing skills (including life skills), building self-confidence, solving problems and developing self-reliance. Education facilitates this process of empowerment, enables boys and girls to question existing inequalities, as well as act for change."[9] Therefore, the above

6. Ibid, 40–55.
7. Rowlands, *Questioning Empowerment*, 13.
8. Vayrynen, *Evidence of empowerment*, 11.
9. UNESCO, *Gender in Educatio*, 26.

information implies that empowerment is about enabling people to take control over their lives, pursuing their own goals, living according to their values, developing self-reliance and being able to make choices and influence both individual and collective decisions which affect their lives.

I will use the word empowerment to show how women can be enabled to participate in education, as well as the social, economic and decisions-making which affect their lives and society at large. Since participation requires increased influence and control it also demands increased empowerment in educational, social, and economic. My focus is how women are enabled by Ushirika wa Neema to participate in economical and social activities to improve their own lives and position or status in the Chagga patriarchal society. This study will not focus on political empowerment because deaconess centre—Ushirika wa Neema which is my case study—does not deal with political issues. Once women are empowered educationally, socially and economically, however, they have an impact on power relations between men and women. Empowerment makes it possible to analyze power inequality and oppressions in Chagga patriarchal society, with the emphasis on enabling women to have power and influence over social and economic decision-making in and outside the households.

By using the word power I mean the overall position of women in a society and the autonomy which they possess as well as how they are free of men's control which marginalizes them. I look at power through the lens of both men and women sharing equally in distribution of power and influence: they should have equal opportunities for financial independence through work or setting up businesses and enjoy equal access to education and opportunities to develop personal ambitions. To achieve this balance of power woman should be empowered to have more autonomy to manage their lives. Chapter six shows how Ushirika wa Neema Deaconess Centre contribute to the empowerment of women in ELCT-Northern diocese and how this empowerment has contributed to improving women's status in the church and society.

Third-Wave Feminism and Empowerment Theories

Origin of the Empowerment Approach

According to Stromquist[10] who studied the origin of the word empowerment, revealed that the concept of empowerment was originally used in United States during the civil rights movement in the 1950s up to the 1960s. It was used to advocate for the elimination of laws which separated black African Americans from white Americans.[11] However, the concept of empowerment is used in the women's movement to oppose gender inequalities in the society.[12] Feminists have developed various theories out of it such as Women in Development (WID) and Gender and Development (GAD).

Woman in Development (WID) is a concept which is based on the recognition that women play important roles in the development process. The WID approach, however, does not necessarily result in changing male-female hierarchical gender relations. Rather, it intends to support women-specific practical needs, such as women's skills development for income generation.[13] In 1970s WID emphasized on including women in development. Since the intervention of including women in development was from top—down, it failed.

Gender and Development (GAD) focuses on intervention to address unequal gender relations in the entire development cycle (access, processes and outcomes) that prevent women from full and equal participation in, and benefits from, development. GAD is a concept developed out of lessons learnt from the experiences gained through WID programmes and activities. It seeks to have both women and men participate, make decisions and share benefits. This approach emphasizes long-term strategic concerns in order to reach the ultimate goal of gender equality.[14]

---

10. Stromquist, *The Theoretical and Practical Bases for Empowerment*, 13–22.
11. Ibid.
12. Oduyoye, *Who Will Roll the Stone Away?* 45–50.
13. UNESCO, *Gender in Education*, 26.
14. UNESCO, *Gender in Education*, 26.

The first wave feminism and the second wave feminism used the concept of empowerment to include women in development. The first wave feminism started in the 19th Century. It focused on women in United States of America and Europe. The main objective was to struggle for acquiring women political rights, particularly right to vote.[15] The second wave feminism started in the 1960s. It promoted the liberation and rights of women to own property. It influenced the establishment of marital rape laws, divorce laws, sexual harassment policies in working places.[16]

The feminists believed that to improve women situation there was a need of including them in developmental projects and programmes. The concept of empowerment is often used in a situation of oppression and subordination because empowerment seeks to eliminate the existence and effects of unjust inequalities.[17]

Empowerment Views and Power as Processes of Human Relations

Empowerment is associated with power. It is used to analyze and critique power inequality and oppressions in society. Rowland classified power into four categories.[18]

1. The first category of power is known as *power over*: This is a controlling power exercised between powerful and powerless. It often excluded marginalized groups in decision-making. It promotes inequalities in the society and makes subordinated group respond with resistance or manipulation.

2. The second category of power is identified as *Power to*: This is also known as generative or productive power. It allows actors to exercise their agency for their interests. There is no domination; people are free to make decision about their

15. Ibid.
16. Mason, *Feminism movement*, 17.
17. Rowlands, *Questioning Empowerment*, 20–25.
18. Ibid.

own lives. It creates new possibilities which enable people to access the freedom of making-decision and choice.

3. The third category of power is *power with*: This is a kind of power which emphasizes a collective strength based on support, solidarity and collaboration for members' benefits. In this category, the powerless collaborate to tackle their problems together.

4. The fourth category of power is *power from within*: this is the spiritual strength and uniqueness that exists in each one of us and makes us truly human. It isbased on self-acceptance as well as self-respect which leads to respect for and acceptance of other as equals.

Patriarchal cultures which dominate women and give them secondary status represent **power over**.[19] According to Rhoda many decisions in Tanzania, including decisions about women's own lives, are made by men. Thus men are regarded as decision-makers in many aspects. She states: "Women are not given chance to speak up, especially in the traditional meetings."[20] Kurubai observed that many societies and dioceses in Tanzania had a perception that men are the ones who should rule the society.[21] Thus women are neglected and given secondary status. In most part of Africa women are still controlled by men. Women empowerment is the vital tool in this case to enable them to have **power to or productive power** which increases their ability to resist and challenge **power over**. According to King[22], empowerment is a new understanding of power where power is not practiced in a dominant, hierarchical mode as **power over**. Such power is finite and cannot be shared; only some people can have it, while others remain without it. But power understood as **enabling power**, as empowerment that can be shared, and can grow and increase so that all who participate in it are strengthened and affirmed without

19. King, *Feminist Theology*, 15–20.
20. Rhoda, *Prostitution, Culture And Church*, 11.
21. Kurubai, *From Doubt to Acceptance*, 8.
22. King, *Feminist Theology*, 18.

excluding or diminishing anyone. So, empowerment is about enabling, equipping and giving ability in order to bring changes and promote the balance of power.

The powerless who are often oppressed should collaborate and work together to find some approaches to gain power since power will not be granted to them by just asking it from the powerful class.[23] Women in different societies have established different associations which bring them together to discuss the solutions of their problems, particularly patriarchal practices which oppress them. This has empowered women economically, socially, culturally and spiritually. It fosters gender awareness and disseminates information on women's rights in the society. This will be discussed in detail in chapter six.

When the concept of empowerment is applied in relations to **power with**, **power to** and **power within**, participation is the key aspect which happens.[24] Rowlands argues that within 'power to' and 'power with' descriptions of power and empowerment is concerned with the process by which people become aware of their own interests and interests of others so that both may have greater participation and influence decisions. This is what Oduyoye called partnership and solidarity between men and women. Both men and women should have an equal chance to participate and influence decisions in the family and church: "Solidarity is walking hand in hand, and developing strength through unity so that common interests are protected and common aims are achieved."[25]

Components of Women's Empowerment

Karl identified three components of empowerment of women namely: awareness, capacity—building and participation.[26] The first component to take place when women are empowered

---

23. Ibid.
24. Rowlands, *Questioning Empowerment*, 20–25.
25. Oduyoye, *Who Will Roll the Stone Away?*, 43.
26. Karl, *Women and Empowerment*, 95.

Third-Wave Feminism and Empowerment Theories

is awareness of women issues, gender discrimination, female education, women rights and available opportunities in the society. This aspect is discussed in detail in chapter six on how women's seminars and education offered at Ushirika wa Neema promote awareness among the women in Chagga patriarchal society.

The second component of women's empowerment is capacity-building and learning of important skills and techniques of life: the ability to plan and organize projects or business activities and to contribute to the society. The third component of women empowerment is being able to participate in decision-making inside and outside the household. In chapter six these components are employed to indicate how women from different parishes learned different skills of life at Ushirika wa Neema and the ability to influence decision-making inside and outside home.

Women Empowerment

According to Firdous and Maheen women's empowerment varies from one context to another.[27] But the common aspects of women's empowerment are to enable women to have independent autonomy and control over resources and enable them to participate in decision-making inside and outside the household. Furthermore, women's empowerment is a state of enabling women to be critical and conscious about external realities and aware of their internal thought construction and belief systems that affect their well being in terms of gender justice and social justice, as well as the determination to use their physical, intellectual emotional and spiritual resources to protect their lives and sustain values that guarantee gender equality at personal, social, economic, political and institutional level.[28] Writing in the same vein King argues that Third World women have become empowered to speak to one another, to their communities, they are responding to the challenges

---

27. Firdous and Maheen, *Mapping Women's Empowerment*, 10.
28. Bheemarasetty, *Women's empowerment*, 20.

of their own situation and are taking on change after initiating themselves.[29]

Furthermore, women's empowerment should enable women to perceive themselves as capable and free to make decisions. It involves undoing negative social constructions, so that women can realize that they have the capacity and the right to act and influence decisions. Also, Rowlands discusses three important dimensions of empowerment which are shown in the figure below:

Figure 1: The Three Dimensions of Empowerment

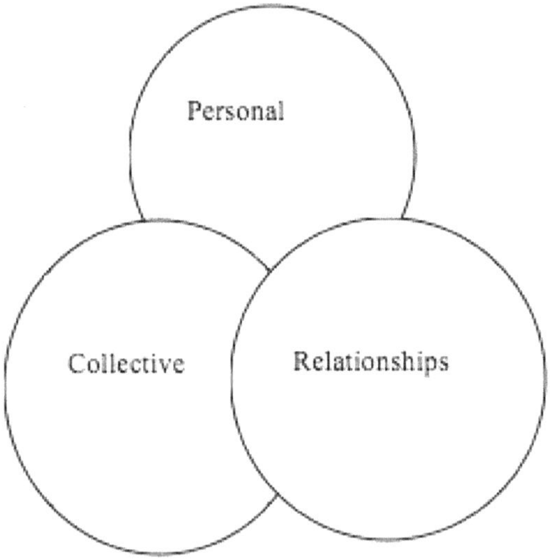

Source: Rowlands.[30]

The above figure shows how empowerment operates within three dimensions which are discussed below as follows:

---

29. King, *Feminist Theology*, 15–20.
30. Rowlands, *Questioning Empowerment*, 14.

Third-Wave Feminism and Empowerment Theories

Personal Dimension

This dimension focuses on individuals. It promotes the development of a sense of self and individual confidence, capacity and undoing of internalized oppressive cultures.[31] This implies that women should be empowered to have individual confidence and capacity to counter oppressive cultures which marginalized them.

Relational Dimension

According to Rowlands, relationship dimension deals with developing the ability to negotiate and influence the nature of a relationship and decisions made within it.[32] This means that women should be empowered in order to have the ability to influence their choices, interests and decisions in the relationships in which they engaged. They should not be passive and receive orders in relationships. They should be enabled to be active participants in making decisions in relationships. In line with this argument, Oduyoye argues that: "for me, the real disease in human relationships is rooted in the perverse patriarchalization of life[33]". She insists upon the importance of empowering African women to speak about their oppressions instead of men doing so on their behalf when she says: "do not let African men tell you that African women do not need to speak of oppression, nor allow them to define what the real source of oppression for African women is[34]". Her argument here is that, there ought to be a separation of men's and women's interests and explanations of issues. For her a person who sleeps on fire is the one who knows the pain of heat. Furthermore, Oduyoye observed that in any relationships in which African women engage, she is placed at lower level due to the hierarchies of patriarchy. This has undermined African women and causes them to lack autonomy. Their identity is completely constructed in relationship to others.

31. Ibid, 14–17.
32. Ibid.
33. Oduyoye, *Feminist Theology*, 54.
34. Oduyoye, *Christian Feminism*, 442.

This makes women's empowerment vital to foster mutual relationship. As Oduyoye states that "God created women and men equally human, made them stewards of creation and gave them authority to manage it jointly.[35]

Collective Dimension

The third dimension of empowerment is collective. This deals with group work which leads to a more achievement rather than individual alone. Collective action may be locally focused, for example groups acting at the village or neighbourhood level or at a more institutionalized level such as activities within national networks.[36] Therefore, collective empowerment helps marginalized women in villages to form entrepreneurial groups for running small businesses. This helps them to develop skills and capacity to control their lives without infringing the rights of others. This agrees with McWhirter who defines empowerment as:

> " *The process by which people, organizations or groups who are powerless (a) become aware of the power dynamics at work in their life context, (b) develop the skills and capacity for gaining some reasonable control over their lives, (c) exercise this control without infringing upon the rights of others and (d) support the empowerment of others in the community.*"[37]

The above definition makes it clear that empowerment is not about gaining the power to dominate others. It also shows that once an individual or group is empowered should also facilitate the empowerment of other marginalized groups and individuals in the community. This will be discussed in details in chapter six to show how deaconesses at Ushirika wa Neema are empowered and use their skills to empower women in the community.

---

35. Oduyoye, *Who Will Roll the Stone Away?* 50–60.
36. Rowlands, *Questioning Empowerment*, 14–20.
37. McWhirter, *Empowerment in Counselling*, 15.

Third-Wave Feminism and Empowerment Theories

Some researchers have reported that empowerment is used in the context of oppressions, because the main aim of empowerment is to remove oppressions and effects of unjust inequalities in the society.[38] Also Rowlands further argues that empowerment can be used on a micro scale that is, connecting people who are experiencing similar situations through self-help, education, social action groups and network building. Empowerment can also be used on a larger scale through community organizations, campaigns, social planning and policy development. The next part explores how women can be empowered economically and educationally.

Economic Empowerment

Economic empowerment entailed that women should be enabled to take part in economic activities such as business and projects which enable them to have some degree of financial independence.[39] The government of Tanzania seems to promote the economic empowerment of women through establishment of small and medium female enterprises. This is facilitated by increasing women's access to financial services such as credit, training in entrepreneurship, training in business management, and access to markets.[40] Additionally, Mgossi shows how the government of Tanzania has being supporting the economic empowerment of women:

> Efforts are being engaged by the government of Tanzania to enable women to gain standard certification of their products and increased access to both local and foreign markets. For instance, the National Micro-Finance Policy, like most recent policies, presents opportunities and provisions for gender equity, states on its paragraph 3.2.5, "access to financial services should be available to both men and women." Moreover, it also urges that it

---

38. Rowlands, *Questioning Empowerment*, 14–20.
39. Karl, *Women and Empowerment*, 65.
40. Ibid, 3.

might be "necessary to make special efforts to incorporate features that make the services accessible to all."[41]

Thus, it seems as if the Tanzanian government is modifying its financial policies in order to enable women to access financial services for their small projects and business. In line with this argument the National Micro-Finance Policy, which was introduced by Tanzanian government in 2000, provides guidelines to foster gender equity in accessing financial services in order to empower women economically. It creates the platform that enables both men and women to access financial services.[42] The Policy also gives flexibility in regulating micro-finance institutions and motivates such institutions to provide credit to women on terms and conditions that can be afforded by the women. Thus, the government of Tanzania has endeavoured to mobilize women in various communities to form Savings and Credit Cooperative Associations (SACCOs) and Community Banks.

Despite the efforts made by the government of Tanzania to enable women to have access in the financial services some studies show that women in Tanzania who have access to financial services from banks is less than 8%.[43] Besides the difficult conditions and terms, the majority of women cannot afford to pay the costs which are involved in processing their loans. Mgossi argues that the majority of women borrow the money to run their small businesses and projects from micro-credit organizations.[44] According to the experiences of microfinance in Tanzania the majority of women have higher repayment rates compared to men.[45]

Moreover, the document known as "Private Sector Development Strategy for Tanzania" provides some vital suggestions for empowering women to have access to the markets. The document focuses on promoting economic empowerment of women in

---

41. Ibid.
42. URT, *Country Report*, 9.
43. Mgossi, *Women's Economic Empowerment in Tanzania*, 1–6.
44. Ibidi, 3.
45. Ibid.

business. Some of the strategies suggested by Private Sector Development Strategy for Tanzania are: "Addressing the legal, administrative and regulatory barriers that are preventing women from contributing fully to the economy. Eliminating gender based inequalities in education and access to agricultural inputs with a view to increasing the contribution of women to growth and addressing the barriers specifically facing women owned enterprises."[46]

The Tanzanian government has realized the importance of including women in development of the nation. In order to do so, the government of Tanzania has decided to eliminate all barriers which prevent women from contributing fully to the economy of the country.

In addition, in Tanzania women to some extent have been economically empowered to participate in international and local trade fairs and exhibitions, through which they have been able to market their products as well as gain and learn from each other on marketing and product development.[47] By doing so the Tanzanian women acquires skills and experiences from other traders in both national and international markets. These experiences may contribute to confidence-building among women and enabling them to face the challenges of competition and globalization. This increases their respect and status in the church and community.

Women should be empowered economically in order to get access to better jobs and higher wages. Studies have shown that when women hold asserts or gain income, the money is more likely to be spent on nutrition, medicine and housing and consequently their children will be healthier.[48] There is evidence to suggest that for every dollar a woman earns, she invests 80 cents in her family. Men, on the other hand, invest around 30 cents and are likely to squander money on alcohol and other vices.[49] Also, Anuratha argues that women who have education and access to income have more bargaining power within their families, and also

46. Mgossi, *Women's Economic Empowerment*, 6.
47. URT, *Country Report*, 10.
48. Ibid.
49. Ibid.

have greater say in spending household income than uneducated and unemployed women.[50]

Although African women produce around 70 percent of food crops, as shown in chapter two, they receive about 5 percent less of the agricultural training and tools available to men.[51] In line with this argument Seitei argues that women are still marginalized in the community.[52] Women in rural areas have long working hour under difficult circumstances such as heat, rain and without proper technologies to ease the work load. The U.N. Report[53] suggests that if women are empowered to access education, training, and given modern equipment, they could produce 20 to 30 percent more crops.

Learning of Skills to Set Up Businesses and Projects

Economic empowerment enables women to set up businesses and projects in their organizations. This encourages them to know that they are capable. As Rowlands states that, "As women form their organizations and work together it enables them to move forward confidently from the concept 'we cannot' to the positive change 'we can.'"[54] She further insists that there is a strong focus on the collective dimension as an adjunct to personal empowerment. She asserts that: "from a state of powerless that manifests itself in a feeling of 'I cannot' empowerment contains an element of collective self-confidence that results in a feeling of 'we can.'"[55] In such organizations, women acquire skills which raise their consciousness to help one another in order to improve their standard of living. In this case Rowlands claims that: "New forms of con-

---

50. Anuratha, *Gender Equality and Development*, 8.
51. Ibid.
52. Seitei, *Areas of weaknesses*, 10.
53. Ibid.
54. Rowlands, *Questioning Empowerment*, 22–23.
55. Ibid, 23.

Third-Wave Feminism and Empowerment Theories

sciousness arise out of women's newly acquired access to the tangible resources of analytical skills, social networks, organizational strength, solidarity and sense of not being alone."[56] Hence, women acquire income in their organizations which enable single mothers to provide basic needs for their children as discussed below.

Independent Income

Kanyoro points out that women's organization in different societies and churches have helped single mothers and women to access independent income which enables them to perform activities which are regarded as men's roles.[57] For instance when women participate in small businesses they accumulate money which enables them to pay school fees for their children, build houses, and pay for health services. This agrees with Moser[58] who argues that women's employment through small businesses and projects influences changes in patriarchal society as women are able to control material resources and non-material resources. She further says: "*Women's empowerment is the capacity of women to increase their own self-reliance and internal strength.*"[59] Therefore, the empowerment of women is important to enable women to have independent autonomy and control over resources and enable them to participate in decision-making inside and outside the household.

However, the ability to exercise control can vary from person to person and from situation to situation. Thus, the empowering environment plays a key role in promoting changes in women's lives and their ability to be employed. The government of Tanzania has formulated some employment documents to foster equality between men and women in the workplaces. Despite efforts made by the government and the church to enable women to get

---

56. Ibid, 22.
57. Kanyoro, *Introducing Feminist Cultural Hermeneutics*, 22.
58. Moser, *Gender Planning in the Third World*, 17–23.
59. Ibid, 19.

employment in the formal and informal sectors, they still have a burden of domestic duties as explained in detail in the next section.

Women's Employment and Domestic Duties

The Employment and Labour Relations Act [2003] of Tanzania, promotes equal opportunities to women and men. It does not allow discrimination practices at work places. The Employment and Labour Relations Act also provides protection to pregnant female employees through social security. More than 30% of job seekers who have visit the Public Labour Exchange Centres since their establishment in 2002 are women.[60]

Furthermore, the government is promoting the empowerment of women through provision of information to women about different jobs and advising them on job availability and other opportunities launched by the National Gender Machinery. However, this does not mean women get employment easily; still there are some patriarchal challenges which hamper women employment especially transforming the mindsets of some governmental and private sector employers who do not promote women's employment and equality between men and women in the workplaces.[61]

On the other hand, women are employed in informal and formal sectors but continue to bear the main burden of domestic duties. Women often participate in the economic activities at the same time performing the domestic activities.[62] Unfortunately, their housework contribution is not recognized as formal economic activity and is not regarded as important in the realm of economic growth and development.[63] Omari points out that "perhaps the most serious deficiency in the statistics regarding women's labour is that a large number of workers simply are not accounted

---

60.
61. Ibid, 2.
62. Oduyoye, *Who Will Roll the Stone Away?*, 55–60.
63. Omari C.K. *Rural Women, Informal Sector,* 19–22.

for at all."[64] This perspective is discussed in detail in chapter six by analyzing the distribution of work at home and outside home after women acquire skills for life from Ushirika wa Neema and establish small businesses and projects.

Educational Empowerment

Education is a basic human right to which every person is entitled. Therefore, education is important for everyone, but it is particularly significant for girls and women.[65] This is due to the fact that education is one among the significant means of empowering women with the knowledge, skills and self-confidence which are very essential to participate fully in the development process. Education helps girls and women to know their rights and to gain confidence to claim them. However, women's literacy rates are significantly lower than men's in most developing countries.[66] So, educational empowerment is useful for developing critical consciousness of women's circumstances and the social environment that leads to action.

Importance of Educational Empowerment

Educated mothers are more likely to be employed, allowing them to pay some of the costs of schooling and being more aware of the benefits of schooling. And educated mothers, averaging fewer children, can concentrate more attention on each child. Besides having fewer children, mothers with schooling are less likely to have mistimed or unintended births.[67] Mahmud et al[68] observe that women's subordination to men fostered and sustained a high fertility which was beneficial to male patriarchs. Female education

64. Ibid, 20.
65. Donnelly, *Universal Human Rights,* 3.
66. UNFPA, *Understanding gender,* 12.
67. Ibid.
68. Mahmud, S. *Women's Empowerment,* 1–5.

education and paid work play a great role in reducing women's subordination to men within the household. This empowerment improved their decision-making role and agency in regulation and child survival. The Mahmud et al write: "Thus an enhancement in women's position was seen as the pathway through which improvements in women's status attained through schooling and paid work, could affect reproductive behaviour."[69]

The above excerpt seems to indicate that the empowerment of women raises the status of women in the church and society. May be respect for women increase because when they are educated and employed they can earn income and support financially the education of their children and other family needs. This empowerment has implications for schooling, because poor parents often must choose which of their children to educate.

There is evidence to suggest that the choice is often made on the basis of gender as Rose and Tembon have reported: *If the parents have three or four children, they would only send one of their children to school because they cannot afford to pay school expenses for all of them . . . since they look down on girls, they prefer to send boys to school.*[70]

The above assertion shows that if women are educated and empowered they will also be a source of income for the family. They will contribute to the payment of schools fees for their children. This empowerment will increase the number of girls with access to education, hence raising the standard of living of the family. This concept is discussed in detail in chapter six. However, Malcolm X insists that "if you educate a man you educate one person but if you educate a woman you liberate and educate the whole nation". He further argues:

> If you are in a country that is progressive, the woman is progressive. If you are in a country that reflects the consciousness toward the importance of education, it's because the woman is aware of the importance of education. But in every backward country you will find

69. Ibid, 2.
70. Rose, and Tembon, "*Girls and Schooling,* 95.

women are backward, and in every country where education is not stressed it's because the women don't have education.[71]

The above assertion implies that female education is very powerful for bringing positive changes to a society and fosters the mechanism of eliminating the poverty in the nation. Therefore, education is the most valuable gift that parents can give to their daughters. Once a woman is educated she would be able to participate in the day-to-day activities of the family. This education would only add up one more voice and an opinion. An educated mother would be more conscious about the health and hygiene of the family than her illiterate counterpart.

In order to empower female education, the government of Tanzania has improved the education sector in order to reduce gender disparity in the education system from primary schools to university. The aim is to empower women to acquire education like men. For example, the Primary Education Development Programme (PEDP) (2001–2006) abolished school fees in primary education.[72] By doing so the enrolment of girls in primary schools increased. Also the government of Tanzania promotes the enforcement of by-laws and regulations which promote the enrolment and retention of female students in the schools. This practice is useful to enable female students to be more likely to complete school.

In order to influence gender awareness in the societies and the enrolment of girls, the government of Tanzania decided to produce information, education and communication materials which are used to sensitise the parents, schools, and societies on enrolment and retention of girls in schools. To ensure access to education for the girls a special fund for girls has been established by Ministry of Education and Culture to support female education. It is known as Girls' Secondary Education Support Programme (GSES). In this programme 2,980 girls benefited from it between 1998 and 2002.[73]

71. Malcolm X, http://www.malcolm-x.org/quotes.htm.
72. URT, *Country Report*, 15.
73. Ibid, 16.

Empowerment and Autonomy of Women

In addition, the government of Tanzania is promoting the empowerment of women through establishment of some schemes which enhance females access to higher studies in colleges and universities. For example, at the University of Dar es Salaam, a programme has been established to enhance girls' access to university education. Girls are assisted by being given remedial classes in order to improve their performance and retention in science and mathematics subjects.[74] Not only this but also there is a Female Undergraduate Scholarship programme, in which development partners have complemented government efforts by sponsoring female students at the university to mitigate the burden of costs. The programme enhances the capacity of the University of Dar-es- Salaam to promote gender mainstreaming with improved female education. As a result of these programmes female students enrolled at the University of Dar esSalaam in 2001 constituted 27 percent and increased to 28 percent in 2003. In Zanzibar, the proportion of female students in the public universities was 34 percent in 2003 while in private universities the proportion reached 49 percent in the same year.[75]

The government of Tanzania is trying to eliminate the stereotypes in teaching materials and textbooks in the education sector. Teaching methodologies have been modified and teachers are introduced to gendered classroom interactions. Furthermore, gender courses have been established in institutions of some higher learning institutions like colleges and universities.[76] Moreover, women are encouraged to join vocational training institutions to learn different skills, which have enhanced their performance, as well as improved women status and increased the value to the jobs which women pursue in the Small and Medium Enterprises (SMEs) and informal sector.[77]

Regardless of the discussed above achievements, the traditional gender stereotyped roles and patriarchal cultures continue

74. Ibid.
75. Ibid, 14 -15.
76. Ibid.
77. Ibid, 15–16.

to hamper women's access to formal education, especially in higher institutions of learning like universities and colleges. In addition, the lack of financial resources and early marriages are other factors which prevent girls from accessing higher education. Another challenge is to motivate girls to pursue vocational training courses which are perceived as male-dominated and for long time have been considered as training only for men and boys. Therefore, the majority of girls and women have been left out of the mainstream of vocational training. Thus, women who join vocational training colleges offering non-traditional skills such as plumbing, mechanics and masonry, are still very few.

Education and Women Leaders

There is a perception that education plays a key role to enable educated female to be leaders.[78] It assumed that women leaders tend to be inclusive and collaborative.[79] On the other hand, Chandler[80] points out that there are gender prejudice constructions between women and men leadership. According to her, women leaders are associated with communal qualities of compassion, affection, gentleness and men are associated with qualities of self-confidence and dominance.

In my view each feminist theory should be perceived within the contextual framework of empowerment. Third Wave Feminist theories and concepts of women empowerment function differently in a diversity of contexts. In context above, the third wave feminist theories and empowerment approaches are relevant. The following chapter analyzes how third wave feminist theories and empowerment approaches are used by Ushirika wa Neema to promote the empowerment of women in Evangelical Lutheran Church in Tanzania—Northern Diocese.

---

78. Blyth, & Wend, *No Boundaries to Compassion*, 19.
79. Chandler, *What women bring to the exercise of leadership?* 1–12.
80. Ibid.

CHAPTER 6

The Empowerment of Women by *Ushirika wa Neema* Deaconess Centre

Introduction

THE PREVIOUS CHAPTER DISCUSSES Third-Wave Feminism and the empowerment theories which are relevant to this study. Third-Wave feminism is a feminist movement which involves economic, political, social, and personal empowerment of women. Also, it focuses more on the individual empowerment of women than on activism. It promotes women to build meaningful identities in the complex contemporary world. Third-Wave feminism encourages personal empowerment and action as a starting point for promoting changes in the society. Also, in the previous chapter I examined the concept of women's empowerment which focuses on enabling women to take control over their lives, pursuing their own goals, living according to their values, developing self-reliance and being able to make choices and influence both individual and collective decisions which affect their lives.

In this chapter, I present analyses of the data. Accordingly, the main purpose of this book is to investigate how Ushirika wa Neema Deaconess Centre contributes to the empowerment of women in the Evangelical Lutheran Church in Tanzania—Northern Diocese.

The Empowerment of Women by *Ushirika wa Neema*

I am especially concerned with the work it performs and the way it engages in the local community in order to facilitate empowerment of women within the movement as well as in the local community. The second purpose is to examine the challenges which the deaconesses at Ushirika wa Neema face in the Chagga patriarchal society. Although the deaconess centre has been supported by the church, it is also clear that the work of the Centre and the empowerment of women by some could be seen as being in conflict with cultural traditions and social practices in the Chagga society, especially with regard to the more patriarchal habits and attitudes.

The empowerment of women is explored in two perspectives. The first perspective is how Ushirika wa Neema contributes to the empowerment of women in the church and society. The second perspective explores how Ushirika wa Neema Deaconess Centre empowers its deaconesses. Also here I have looked at issues such as education and economy, as well as addressing how their relation to family is challenged. Therefore, this book will enable people to know the contribution of Ushirika wa Neema Deaconess Centre to the empowerment of women in the church and society which has raised awareness to church and government leaders of gender issues as they also declared that gender is a sensitive issue for the development of Tanzania. This chapter will show how empowered women support the education of their children and other development and projects in the church and society.

Contribution of Ushirika wa Neema towards Empowerment of Women

Ushirika wa Neema contributes to the empowerment of women in the church and society in different ways.

Learning Skills of Life

The issue of empowerment of women is important in the work of the deaconesses. They understand their role as contributing to this. I asked them how Ushirika wa Neema (UWN) Deaconess Centre contributes to the empowerment of women in the church and community. The majority of deaconesses who were interviewed reported that different women groups visit UWN in order to learn important life skills and techniques such as: gardening, animal keeping, cooking varieties of food and establishing women entrepreneurs. The Mother of the deaconesses expressed it thus:

> *Many women groups who have visited Ushirika wa Neema acquired skills and initiated small projects and businesses. However, these small projects and businesses have little capital because of the inability to generate a high amount of savings. In order to generate credit for running their businesses, women have formed an informal credit system. They call it Upatu or kibati, in which they lend each other money in turns so as to accumulate cash to start small businesses. By doing so, they have initiated cow projects, pig project, retail shops, cooking groups which are given venues to cook and decorate in various ceremonies like weddings, baptisms, confirmation ceremonies and burial services. They get good breeds of cattle which produce 15 -20 litres of milk per day compared to local breeds which produce 2–3 litres of milk per day. Through these groups, women are learning how to organize business. Thus women are being empowered as they participate in these activities.*[1]

The above quotation implies that the teaching of life skills and techniques help both individual woman and women's groups in different parishes to establish various projects such as: gardening, animal keeping, catering and entrepreneurs. This teaching of skills and techniques of life seems as an important way for the deaconesses to increase the empowerment of women in the church and society. The learning of different skills makes them more independent. They can to larger extent be self-reliant, just as Rowlands states: "Empowerment is a process whereby women become able to organize themselves to increase their own self-reliance, to assert their independent right to make choice and to control resources

1. Informant 1.

which will assist them to challenge and eliminate their own subordinations."[2]

The above quotation indicates that when a woman is empowered economically she is able to be self-reliant and control resources without depending on her husband. As I said earlier in chapter five collective empowerment helps marginalized women in villages to form groups for running small businesses and entrepreneurs. This collective empowerment helps them to develop skills and capacity to control their lives without infringing upon the rights of others.

Access to Independent Income

UWN contributes to empower women to access independent income which help them to improve their standard of living in the society. They can pay school fees, make church contributions and help needy people. Deaconess 10 said: "*My sister has one son. She is not married. She had a problem of paying the school fees of her son. Since she came here and learned to run a pig project and get a good breed, she is now paying the school fee without a problem and she has started to build a house with bricks.*"[3]

The above statement shows that the skills acquired by women groups in terms of running small projects seemed to help single mothers and women in the society to build houses, as well as paying school fees for their children and health services. This aspect also implies that when women are empowered economically they seemed to perform activities which traditionally are regarded as the role of men. For example, after acquired skills from UWN on how to organize small projects she managed to build a house with bricks. This view agrees with Kanyoro who argues:

> Women do not thatch houses because they don't have money. That makes it to be man's duty. If a man has lots of wives and does not like some, he just refuses to repair

---

2. Rowlands, *Questioning Empowerment*, 17.
3. Informant 10.

the roofs of the houses belong to the wives who have fallen out of favour. He may also refuse to repair the roof of an only wife to punish her for some reason or other. But in most cases, men move out to work in the cities. They earn very little money and can only come home in six months. Then it is very hard for the wife and children if the rains come and house leaks. Through small business women accumulate their little profits and thatch their houses with iron roof.[4]

Therefore, women who engage in doing small businesses accumulate their little profits and built houses as well as providing financial support to society and church.

Furthermore, informant 8 explained how they share their earnings with marginalized people in the society and contribute to their parishes as a way of thanking God for giving them income. She comments:

> Even though our income is small, if you spend it properly it is enough and we can help the needy people to some extent. We thank and praise God when we compare ourselves with other women who are not employed or do not have self-employment. Here we cannot get extra income to save, but the small income we get we share with others and contribute to some extent to our church. We are satisfied to some extent. It would be selfish if we do not share with others what we earn.[5]

This informant revealed that some of the women who acquired skills from UWN seemed to engage in small businesses and have access to income and credit. They seemed to be very careful in spending their income. They allocate portion of their earnings to the needy people in the society. This might help particularly those who are living vulnerable lives to meet to some extent their basic needs like food and clothes. This view agrees with McWhirter who defines empowerment as: "The processes by which people or group of people that are powerless are empowered and support

4. Kanyoro, *The Power we Celebrate*, 22.
5. Informant 8.

the empowerment of others in the community."[6] It also shows that once an individual or group is empowered they also facilitate the empowerment of other marginalized groups and individuals in the community.

Informant 8 points out that they use their small profit to support church activities. This shows that when women access independent income they may provide financial support in their parishes. Writing in the same vein Kanyoro states: "Women continue to raise funds for church use, including subsidies for pastor's salaries. They continue to build community centres for the church out of their own meagre income. Their little offering, equivalent to the widow's mite, is still the most important local income of the church."[7] I agree with Kanyoro that when women are empowered economically they support a lot of church activities. During the field I observed that majority of women participate actively to support diaconal work and charitable services in their societies.

Oduyoye insists that the church is made up of both men and women; therefore, the church should acknowledge that women can contribute positive things to the church and society as men do.[8] Thus, men and women need to learn and appreciate the role played by each other in order to bring a full communion within the body of Christ.

Self-employment

The learning of small projects and businesses at UWN contributes to the empowerment of women through self-employment in the informal sector which raises their status and respect in society and increases the chance of women to participate more in decision-making processes. Deaconess 5 testifies in the following words:

> *Since my sister started to run a small business and new cow breed project, she earns an income which enables her*

---

6. McWhirter, *Empowerment in Counselling*, 15.
7. Kanyoro, *The Power we Celebrate*, 24.
8. Oduyoye M. *Who Will Roll the Stone Away?* 90.

> *to support her family and our parents because my salary goes to my new surrogate communal family at Ushirika wa Neema. When I went home to visit my parents and relatives, I noted that my biological family and neighbours are respecting my sister and consult her for various kinds of advice. Now, she is able to advise her husband. For example she shared with me that she has advised him to take a loan from SACCOS to pay the school fees of their daughter. They are now paying it slowly by instalments.*

It seemed that once women are empowered economically, they might be able to access funds and handle some family matters. This raises their status and respect in the society. Also, they can have generative power which is discussed in chapter five. This generative power helps them to influence decision-making in the family. This agrees with Anuratha who argues that women who have education and access to income have more bargaining power within their families, and also have greater say in spending household income than uneducated and unemployed women.[9]

Additionally, information from the fifth deaconess seemed to indicate that training offered by deaconesses to women's groups contributes to some extent toward the creation of employment opportunities for women in informal sector.[10] Thus, the informal sector becomes a very important source of employment for women in Tanzania. UWN seems to foster women's economical empowerment as it enables them to participate in the small businesses where they are able to carry out some forms of transactions of both farm and non-farm products. This agrees with Karl who argues that women's participate in small businesses leads to "greater wage employment opportunities and more participation in self-employ-

---

9. Anuratha, *Gender Equality and Development,* 8.

10. Informal sector can be defined as the way of doing economic activities consisting of the following elements: (a) easy entry into the economic activities, (b) reliance on indigenous resources—finance and materials, (c) it is a family owned enterprises (d) small scale of operation, (e) labour intensive—depending mainly on family labour and adopted technology, (f) skills to operate the business are required outside the formal school system (g) there exists an unregulated and competitive market (Omari informal *sector 5).*

ment and in the informal sector, which in turn leads to higher productivity, higher wage earnings, more access to credit and higher entrepreneurial earnings."[11] In the same vein the Government of Tanzania has initiated a number of programmes and projects in promoting rural and urban self-employment with emphasis on availing more employment and opportunities to poor women. Labor laws are being reviewed to become more gender sensitive and to enforce safety regulations in the work places for both men and women.[12] Nevertheless, the Employment and Labour Relations Act of 2003 was passed by the Tanzanian Parliament, which prohibits discrimination in the work place on the basis of gender, sex, marital status, disability and pregnancy among others. This law also requires employers to report to the Labour Commissioner on their plans to promote equal opportunities. The law protects employees during pregnancy and women employees by providing social security hence shifting the cost from the employer to the social security fund.[13]

Women's employment through small businesses and projects appears to influence changes in patriarchal society as women are able to control material resources and non-material resources. Writing in the same vein Moser argues that: "Women empowerment is the capacity of women to increase their own self-reliance and internal strength. This is identified as the right to determine choices in life and to influence the direction of change, through the ability to gain control over material and non-material resources."[14]

The quotation above implies that women in patriarchal culture have commenced slowly to recognize the oppressive culture and convince the society to promote the rights of women. In the same vein King argues that women in the lower socio-economic groups are recognizing the benefit of collective action through self-help groups and cooperatives that empower them gradually to rethink their rights and to challenge the structures that keep

11. Karl, *Women and Empowerment*, 9.
12. URT, *Country Report*, 16.
13. Ibid, 17.
14. Moser, *Gender Planning*, 19.

them imprisoned.[15] Oduyoye has reported that this movement of women empowerment and employment is changing gender relations in the church and society. Oduyoye insists that women empowerment promotes the partnership and solidarity of men and women in the church and society.[16]

Thus, some women have noted that when they are generating income from business activities their husbands cannot harass them, because they are able to take care of the family without the husband's financial support. This however does not apply to all women. In some families, when the woman increases in economic power as a result of her participation in such businesses, it leads to serious misunderstandings in their marriages because of the patriarchal culture which maintains 'power over' and extended family system. When the husband assists his wife to carry out some domestic duties, as a result of her wife absence for work, some people in the society consider him as 'controlled by his wife', they use a Swahili saying which says: '*amekaliwa na mke wake*' literary meaning '*his wife sits on him.*' Others say that: '*mke wake amemweka mfukoni*' literary meaning '*his wife has placed him in her pocket*'. This situation discourages men from assisting their wives in performing domestic activities like cooking, house cleaning, feeding children and washing clothes.

Women are now more knowledgeable about resources mobilization, allocation and control. This agrees with Karl who argued that among the significant component which happens when women are empowered economically is capacity-building and learning important life skills and techniques, the ability to plan, organize projects or business activities and contribute to the society.[17] Another component of women's empowerment is being able to participate in decision-making inside and outside the household. It seemed as if such business opportunities which women learn at UWN empower them to influence decisions in their families and the community. This also increases their confidence and

---

15. King, *Feminist Theology*, 109.
16. Oduyoye M. *Who Will Roll the Stone Away?* 37.
17. Karl, *Women and Empowerment*, 9–35.

The Empowerment of Women by Ushirika wa Neema

self-esteem. At this point, one can argue that the deaconesses at Ushirika wa Neema have contributed to some extent in changing the traditional Tanzanian patriarchal society's attitudes of neglecting women, leading to better socialization and relationship between men and women in the church and society. This is also useful to children, who need to grow up with good perceptions toward promoting gender equality. As Oduyoye argues God has created both men and women equally human, and gave them a responsibility of been stewards of the creation and granted them authority to administer it together in good relationship without oppressing each other.[18]

Apart from the economical contributions of UWN to the empowerment of women as seen above one can raise a question: does access to independent income acquired through skills learned from UWN change gender power and relation in the patriarchal society? In this situation we are cautioned that having more self-confidence and dignity do not necessarily lead to changes in how power is exercised or experienced but empowerment is what happens as a result of having self-confidence and dignity.[19] In view of this, Vayrynen argues that even though evidence show that women gain more self-confidence when they engage in businesses and project programmes, this does not means that women's needs or interests have been fulfilled.[20] But this book argues that self-confidence and self-esteem show 'power within women' which influence 'generative power'; this means that women become more aware of their own experiences in life and gain confidence to challenge the patriarchal structure which subordinates them. Hence, it increases the chance of women to participate in decision-making processes.

On the other hand the Principal of the Montessori Training College UWN cautioned that even though women are helped to have individual or collective employment out of the home, they still have to do the domestic activities. She said: *Women who work*

---

18. Oduyoye M. *Who Will Roll the Stone Away?* 86.
19. Rowlands, *Questioning Empowerment*, 127.
20. Vayrynen, *Evidence of empowerment*, 11.

Empowerment and Autonomy of Women

outside the home are still responsible for domestic work of the household which makes them to have a double work burden which is a barrier for better employment opportunities and economic participation in formal and informal sectors. In this respect, women are helped to have individual or collective employment outside home but still they have to do the domestic activities. Even though Ushirika wa Neema Deaconess Centre is promoting women empowerment and participation of women in small projects and businesses still more effort is needed due to the fact that there is still inequalities between women and men.

The Tanzania Country Report on the Millennium Development Goal of 2010 shows that the proportion of females in wage employment remains low as women constitute only 30% of paid employees. Females also spend more time on unpaid care work (15%) compared to 5% for males. This agrees with the case of Nordic women. Pessi, Anne Birgitta state: "Even though Nordic women participate both in politics and labour market they also retain the major responsibility for work in the household."[21]

Similarly, the Tanzania Country Report on the Millennium Development Goal of 2010 states:

> Women's work load still continues to haunt them, working more than 14 hours a day. Absence or inadequate support to home-based care adds to the burden on women. This calls for change of mindset concerning the traditional roles the society has assigned the women. Although in urban areas women are now allowed to participate in decision making, rural areas are still rigid. Risk and vulnerability to HIV and AIDS befall mainly women and girls. Women give care to the sick, the orphans and infected members.[22]

The quotation above indicates that patriarchal culture tends to favor and offer privileges and opportunities to men over women. Even though there is some changes in decision-making after the engagement of women in economic projects offered at Ushirika

21. Pessi, and Anne, *The Churhch*, 81.
22. URT, *Tanzania Country Report*, 23.

The Empowerment of Women by *Ushirika wa Neema*

wa Neema, domestic activities have remained unchanged for the majority of women. Men who assist their wives to perform house activities are still few, and those who try to do that are discouraged by their friends and relatives as discussed earlier. This indicates that there had not been a big change of men' ideas about women roles. In line with this argument Rowlands states: "A woman may become personally empowered in many ways, including becoming able to earn her own living. However, if she continues to carry the full responsibility for domestic duties, including child care, at the same time her 'empowerment' has actually increased her burden. In some cases this is also enables the man to take even less responsibilities than before."[23]

The above excerpt indicates that there is division of labour in domestic chores. Gender roles are constructed by the society and imparted from one person to another through socialization since the childhood. In many African societies some domestic activities like taking care of children, cooking and cleaning are regarded as the role of women. Similarly, Anurather writes that: *"The division of labour in domestic chores and child care is rarely renegotiated across the genders, despite the women increased labour input into paid work; women continue to bear the main burden of domestic work, or share it with other female members of the household, often their daughters."*[24]

To larger extent most women often participate in the economic activities at the same time performing the domestic activities. As noted in chapter two on gender issues, in the Chagga patriarchal society women's housework contribution is not recognized in the formal economic activities and is not regarded as important in the realm of economic growth and development. Also, Omari points out that "perhaps the most serious deficiency in the statistics regarding women's labour is that a large number of workers simply are not accounted for at all."[25]

---

23. Rowlands, *Questioning Empowerment*, 132.
24. Anuratha, *Gender Equality*, 12.
25. Omari, *Rural Women*, 20.

Empowerment and Autonomy of Women

On the other hand, Madsen as cited by Omari conducted a study on women's economic activities in one village in Songea, Southern Tanzania; she found that since economic activities of the women were based on sexual division of labour, their contribution to the village economic process was minimal. As a result she concludes: "Activities concerning women have rather marginal character, and are insufficient in relation to needs. The process is developing slowly and the results are rather poor. Almost all the women's project are based on the traditional sexual division of labour and centre around household activities or extended household activities."[26]

She also argued that International Labour Organization (ILO) has defined the labour force and what constitutes its contribution to the economy, which does not account for people who are not engaged in full time paid work. Thus, when surveys are done on the labour force, women, children, and old people who perform many activities which are economically suitable at household level, do not come to light in the collected data. She further says that even the researchers, being male-dominated tends to some extent to categorize women's activities as housework and domestic rather than economic activities, while the same activities if carried out by men would have been categorized as economic.[27] These are purely sexual and cultural discriminatory attitudes that exist in Chagga patriarchal society. Thus, Fiorenza argues that patriarchal society and culture is characterized by its sexual and economic exploitation of all women which is sustained and legitimised by the cult of the true womanhood, the myth of femininity, romantic love, and education to domesticity.[28]

Moreover, Karl argues that a lack of accurate information and statistics on women's employment and failure to recognize their domestic duties and agricultural activities have resulted in the failure of established policies which can address their needs. Karl thus writes:

26. Ibid, 19.
27. Ibid, 20.
28. Fiorenza, *Waiting-at-Table*, 84–88.

The Empowerment of Women by *Ushirika wa Neema*

> "At the village or community level, an accurate reflection of the contribution of women farmers in statistics will further provide the justification for fundamental changes in policy, plans, and the allocation of agricultural resources so that all farmers, both male and female, benefit. This would effectively remove many of the constraints women farmers face in increasing their productivity."[29]

The above excerpt implies that more efforts are still needed on providing training for women on production of quality products and marketing skills. There is a need to make an investigation on investment opportunities that women can be involved. Obstacles like access to credit should be eradicated in order to foster women's access to credit which will enable them to establish business and different projects. More efforts are still needed to educate women especially in the villages on how to participate as women entrepreneurs in order to foster the elimination of poverty and promote gender equality. The Government of Tanzania aimed at training 20 percent of women entrepreneurs each year. The number of women entrepreneurs trained has been increased but has not reached the 20 percent[30] target. However, the Government still needs to increase its efforts to train more entrepreneurial women to reach the 20 percent goal it had set.

Therefore, the next subsection discusses how Ushirika wa Neema promotes the empowerment of women through provision of Montessori kindergarten training which help women to get employment in various churches' institutions.

Women Montessori Kindergarten Teachers

Ushirika wa Neema promotes women's empowerment by training women to be Montessori kindergarten teachers. Ushirika wa Neema owns Montessori Kindergarten College which trains Montessori kindergarten teachers. It enrols both girls and boys. Informant 3 said: "*Currently 98% are female students while 2% are*

---

29. Karl, *Women and Empowerment*, 6.
30. http://www.tanzania.go.tz/gender.html.

male students." The enrolments rate shown above demonstrates gender inequality in enrolment. Men are extremely few. So in this case this kindergarten college seems promoting female enrolment as against male counterparts. This raises some issues of concern; is it the case that the women are turning the game against men by refusing more enrolment of males in the school? Or is it due to the fact that the college is considered to be meant for girls or female and that boy do not consider themselves to fit in there? Could it be that the boys consider teaching at kindergarten level as job prescribed for females?

In this scenario, the Mother of deaconess makes it clear that teaching in secondary schools and universities is regarded as male role in patriarchal society while teaching in lower schools like kindergarten and primary is regarded as female role because it is connected with mothering of small children. She said: *"Teaching in secondary schools and universities is regarded as a male role in our community while teaching lower schools like kindergarten and primary is regarded as a female role because it is connected with mothering of small children."*

She further said: *"As far as I am a mother, I know how to take care of the children. The important issues to consider include being polite, kind, and tolerant and not being fast when teaching children."* This view relates with what I pointed out in chapter two that the membership of Evangelical Lutheran Church in Tanzania constitutes more than 50% women but their work in Church activities is very visible at congregational level. They are the ones who oversee the kindergarten owned by the parishes. Women are considered as mothers who are responsible for child-rearing. Therefore, teaching kindergarten and lower classes seemed to be culturally constructed as the role of women. Even though enrolment of boys is very low, the participation of the men in teaching kindergarten is very important because the nurturing and instructions of small children were tasks associated traditionally with mothers within the household sphere. When men participate in the teaching at this level, it reinforces the change of the mindset of patriarchal society that men can also be kindergarten teachers like women. This fosters what Oduyoye[31] called "the partnership and solidarity of men and women." She insists that there is a need for maintaining the partnership and solidarity between men and women, ordained and lay, and this will be the true image of the Church of Christ.[32] Oduyoye spoke these words when she saw the division of unity of the church in the phase of gender, with focus on male and female. She argues that all have been called by God to serve him with different talents which Holy Spirit bestows on us. She insists that we are all created in the image of God and are called to serve God together without undermining one another.[33]

Moreover, the principal of the Montessori Training College at UWN said that women who finished their studies at their college qualify to join diploma studies in social development in public and private colleges. They can upgrade to pursue university studies. She said:

> *Since we started the Montessori program, up to this year 2012 a total of 495 women have graduated at our college. They are employed into different parishes after finishing their Montessori course; they are qualified to pursue diploma studies in social development at public and private colleges. Two women who finished this Montessori programme have upgraded to the extent of joining university studies which will enable them to have better employment and income.*

The excerpt from this informant indicates that there is a perception that education offered at Ushirika wa Neema empowers women to access education at different levels such as certificate course, diploma and university education. In an interview with informant 3, I noted that Montessori kindergarten training offered at Ushirika wa Neema Deaconess Centre raises the respect and status of women in the community as this informant said: "*The women and men at our villages who are not educated like us usually give us much respect because they know our professional jobs*

---

31. Oduyoye, *Who Will Roll the Stone Away?*, 25.
32. Oduyoye, *Introducing African Women's Theology*, 86.
33. Ibid.

that we have the potential to make a contribution in the families and the community. Nowadays my husband does not abuse me." The excerpt from this informant indicates that there is a perception that education offered at Ushirika wa Neema empowers women by increasing women's ability to earn an independent income and increases women's status in the community and leads to greater input into family and community decision making. In line with the above argument Karl argues:

> Education provides girls with a basic knowledge of their rights as individuals and as citizens of their nation and the world. Having knowledge, income and decision making power can place women on a more equal footing with their male counterpart . . . education also provides people with knowledge and skills to contribute to and benefit from development efforts, especially in area of health, nutrition, water and sanitation, and the environment. Efforts in these areas are more likely to be successful if women understand the new concepts and their potential benefits, posses the skills needed to implement new ideas, . . . girls and women education is necessary condition to ensure that development efforts will be sustained.[34]

The above quotation indicates that when women are given education it becomes a tool for promoting sustainable development of the society and nation at large. Thus, when women are empowered through education, gender awareness may flourish as women find employment in parishes and other sectors. Women who have good employment opportunities are mostly financially stable and do not have to depend on their husbands all the time. It also increases their chance to contribute to the household needs, a role that was traditionally left to men in many societies. Moreover, there is a perception that educated woman can control birth rate and provide basic needs to the children compared to illiterate mothers.[35]

---

34. Karl, *Women and Empowerment*, 10.
35. Mahmud, *Women's Empowerment*, 20.

The Empowerment of Women by *Ushirika wa Neema*

When women are given education it enables them to get professional jobs in various sectors. This empowers them to minimize their subordination to men in the household and community.[36] Also, women's participation in education provides a tool to counter those patriarchal cultures which oppress them in the society. This agrees with King Ursula who argues that education plays an important role of raising women's awareness against patriarchal oppression.[37] This also supports Oduyoye, who argues that there is a need for African women to use theological education to liberate themselves from male patriarchy and dominance in both church and society. She believes that women have a crucial role to play to ensure their own rights and liberation.[38] Education is a crucial initial catalyst of feminist theology.

Health and Sexuality

The Centre contributes to promoting women's empowerment though training deaconess sisters who become matrons in different schools and orphanage centres. In this scenario, Informant 2 claims:

> *Dr. Kamm and his wife Dr. Maria Kamm who was the headmistress of Weruweru Girls Secondary School were planning to build a centre for keeping children born by female students at Weruweru Secondary Girls School so that they could continue with their studies; I told them they should not build that centre at that time. Instead I advised them to assist the church to build a Deaconess Sisters Centre so that deaconesses could be the matrons in secondary schools and orphanage centres.*[39]

This view is in agreement with informant 5 who said: "*According to the idea of Dr. Marry Kamm, near to Weruweru Girls*

---

36. Karl, *Women and Empowerment*, 10–15.
37. King, *Feminist Theology*, 5.
38. Oduyoye, *Introducing African Women's Theology*, 80–86.
39. Informant 2.

Empowerment and Autonomy of Women

Secondary Schools there is a centre known as Clementine Foundation which helps girls to accomplish their studies. Deaconess Sister Eva was the first Matron of those girls."[40]

The quotation above shows how UWN is contributing to empower female students to accomplish their studies by providing matrons in different schools and orphanage centres. Clementine orphanage centre takes care of those children so that their mothers can continue schooling and complete their studies.

Usually in the public schools, girls who become pregnant are expelled which severely limits the life options for the girl and undermines her potential contribution to the society. The fear of expulsion forces the girls to have poor performance and also resort to the option of abortion which also threatens their life-span.[41] The main problem as I pointed out in chapter two is that Chagga culture does not allow people to discuss sexual issues openly. Even in schools some teachers are not free to discuss it openly. Therefore, it is necessary for the government to reform the school curriculum in order to introduce health and sex education in both primary education and ordinary secondary education which enable girls to know how to take care of themselves and to avoid pregnancy in school.

Similarly, Larson et al argue that "the need for skill development in the domain of romantic and sexual relationships is one of particular urgency[42]". They further argue: Although sex education is important . . . it seems all the more critical that youth learn skills for managing the intimate relationships in which sexuality occurs. They need educational programs that address feelings, examine choices, cultivate positive skills and reinforce a sense of self worth."[43] In the same vein Geldard and Geldard as cited by Lines caution teachers and parents: "To remember that sexuality is a major and positive dimension of human development. It is important that adolescents come to terms with their sexuality in the ways which are positive. Both teaching and responsible

---

40. Informant 5.
41. Bendera, *Vocational Education 29*.
42. Larson et al, *Adolescents' Preparation*, 56.
43. Ibid, 58.

decision-making and non-judgmental counselling styles have an important role in addressing the casual attitude towards early sex and the rise in teenage pregnancy."[44] The quotations above imply that students should be equipped with skills and knowledge on sexuality through individual and group skill coaching, in order to manage the peer and other kinds of pressure to engage in unsafe sexual practices. Moreover, UWN has ambition of extending their services to university female students.

Aaron Urioh insists:

> *Our aim is not only to help female students at primary and secondary schools only, but we want to extend our service to university female students in Moshi. We are building a hostel which will accommodate 80–100 university girls. Most of them are suffering in the streets with their children. In this women's hostel, deaconess Sisters will be matron(s). We have got a loan of 400 million from Germany for this project. We want also to help students in Katavi in Mpanda region. We have bought a school there; our deaconess sisters will go to render services there. The priority will be to female students.*

The statement above seems to indicate that UWN appears to promote women empowerment through helping University female students though the plan of establishing the female hostel, where deaconesses will become matrons to help the university female students to accomplish their studies on time and get better employment which will help to improve their lives. On the other hand, UWN bought a school in Mpanda region which is located in Southern Tanzania; this is a means of spreading the deaconess ministry to a different part of Tanzania. As far as their priority is to help female students, this increases the access of women to acquire education hence improving their standard of living.

Having discussed how UWN promote female education, the next subsection explores how UWN empowers women through running different women's seminars which are useful to create awareness of women issues, gender discrimination, and women rights.

44. Lines, *Brief Counselling in Schools*, 155.

Empowerment and Autonomy of Women

Organization of Women's Seminars

UWN seems to contribute to the empowerment of women through organizing women seminars. The principal of the Montessori College at Ushirika wa Neema, Mrs. Rev. Aaron Urioh, points out that they usually organize women's seminars every year at Ushirika wa Neema. She is a chairperson of this programme. The focus of these seminars is empowering women. She claimed:

> On 25.06.2012 to 29.06.2012 we conducted a seminar where members were 197 women from all over Tanzania. The themes were: Employment and Labour Relation Laws, Youth and Globalization and Cervical Cancer and Women's Liberation Laws. We also conducted another seminar on 2–8/06/2013 which included all Montessori Kindergarten teachers. We have invited Dr. Eva Maria and two other professors from Sweden as facilitators of this seminar.

The findings show that the themes for the women's seminars at UWN increase awareness about gender issues, and women's rights which sensitizes them to struggle for their justice.

The principal of the Montessori UWN insists: "*Through these seminars we invite women leaders to teach women's rights including widows' inheritance rights because many widows, specifically in the rural areas, do not know their rights. We send announcements of such seminars into our diocese parishes and announce it in our radio Sauti ya Injili so that the information can be disseminated to widows who are active members of our church.*"

The Assistant Chaplain at Ushirika wa Neema comments: "*Through our seminars to women, Ushirika wa Neema brings women together and contributes to the empowering of widows and women in general on how to acquire their rights to land and property.*" This assertion shows that the seminars conducted by Ushirika wa Neema seem to contribute toward empowering women from different parishes all over Tanzania.

As mentioned earlier in chapter four that the first component to take place when women are empowered is awareness of women issues, gender discrimination, and women rights. Such seminars

The Empowerment of Women by *Ushirika wa Neema*

seemed to help women to respond to their contemporary challenges in the patriarchal society such as to challenge oppressive structures in both church and society. However; it is not easy to change a patriarchal system in a short period of time. The themes for the seminars increase their awareness on gender issues and women rights which sensitizes them to struggle for their justice.

Empowerment seminars run at Ushirika wa Neema seemed to help widows from rural areas to know their rights which are advocated in both inheritance laws and women's rights. Also, King argues that if women are not informed of their rights they cannot demand them.[45] As Ushirika wa Neema spreads information on widow and women's rights through seminars, women become more aware of their rights and advocate for a change in the patriarchal society. Through this empowerment seminar, women know the changes which are happening in the constitution and laws. For example Ezer[46] shows that in 2000, Tanzania amended its constitution explicitly to prohibit discrimination on the basis of gender. Tanzania established a committee which deals with implementing the convention on the Elimination of all Forms of Discrimination against Women (CEDAW) which instructed that the allocation of unequal inheritance shares to widow and daughters contravene the convention and should be abolished. This implies that widows should be allowed to inherit their husband's properties. This means that the Tanzanian government has started to reform outdated laws, and particularly inheritance laws. It has also initiated an agenda of promoting the elimination of customs and traditions which affect women negatively. This plays a key role in empowerment of women in Tanzania.

These seminars promote widow empowerment and the spread of knowledge of gender and women rights and thus the structure may change gradually. Such seminars are useful to women for fighting against ignorance and illiteracy which enables them to interrogate patriarchal structure and promote positive changes in

---

45. King, *Feminist Theology*, 5–9.
46. Ezer, *Inheritance Law*, (2002).

the patriarchal society. As Breidlid[47] argues, knowledge is a power which regulates modes of reasoning and supports the possibility for rational and acceptable behaviour regardless of the social and political system. This implies that knowledge which women acquired in the seminars at Ushirika wa Neema may be a powerful for awakening women's consciousness and is a fundamental factor for influencing gender awareness in the society and church.

Contributions of Ushirika wa Neema towards the Empowerment of Deaconesses

Deaconess Educational Empowerment

Ushirika wa Neema participates in the provision of education for deaconesses. Deaconess leaders were asked a question: how do you empower deaconesses at Ushirika wa Neema? Their answers are summarized by the Chaplain's words:

> *We empower deaconess sisters through education. More than 10 deaconess sisters are pursuing their studies in different schools in various professions. This makes them to be the advisers, and counsellors in their societies. They are highly respected and their words are very strong in their families. This is because they are considered as God's servant. They are living the holy life. They have left everything and decided to dedicate their lives to serve Christ.*

On the other hand, Deaconesses were asked the question: How does Ushirika wa Neema empower you as a deaconess? Deaconess 9 said: "*At Ushirika wa Neema all of us are offered the basic training for life.*" She further elaborates the content of this basic training by pointing out that: "*We learn mathematics, domestic science, languages, cookery, agriculture, Christian education, guidance and counselling, ethics and Church history. After the training everyone is allocated into an area of specialization.*" Moreover, Deaconess 6 relates that some of them are sent for further studies in secondary

---

47. Breidlind, *Education, Indigenous Knowledge*, 157.

schools, colleges and universities. The Mother of deaconesses verifies: "*Currently there are more than five deaconesses who are studying secondary education. Three deaconesses are studying a Bachelor's in Education. One deaconess is pursuing a Master's in Education at Mzumbe University. One deaconess has finished her medical studies. She is now working as a medical assistant at Marangu Hospital.*" According to the above excerpt, it can be argued that Ushirika wa Neema Deaconess Center is working hard to empower its deaconess sisters with education in different professionals and levels. Moreover, informant 7 said that:

> *From the beginning of the convent in 1980, the convent management has been looking forward to educating the deaconess sisters in various levels of education and professions, mainly aiming at grooming faithful and committed servants for the church and the community at large. However, after getting education at any level or in any profession, the deaconesses have shown their talents and abilities working hard and faithfully, hence, making a difference wherever they are sent for service. Bearing in mind that they are deaconesses, sisters pursue their studies while focusing on future service that is supported by Christian love, empathy, and sympathy.*

The report (2012) of education development of deaconesses shows that a number of deaconess sisters have pursued different education levels and they have undertaken various professions such as nurses, teachers, pastors, accountants, occupational therapists, veterinarians and agricultural personnel. These sisters do serve mainly in church institutions and in the community at large. The table below shows the educational progress of deaconesses at Ushirika wa Neema.

Education Level	Profession	Number of Sisters
Master's Degree	Accountant	01
Bachelor's Degree	Education/Teaching	04
	Business Admin.	01

Empowerment and Autonomy of Women

Education Level	Profession	Number of Sisters
Diploma	Accountant	01
	Occupational Therapy	01
	Education/Teaching	01
	Child Care/Orphans	02
Clinical Officer	Med. Clinical Officer	01
Secretarial Course	Office Secretary	02
Certificate	Child Caretaker	02
Secondary		07

Source: The report (2012) of education development of deaconesses at Ushirika wa Neema.

Some deaconess sisters are still at different colleges and schools where they are undertaking various courses as it is indicated below:

Table 2: List of courses pursued by deaconesses at various colleges

Education Level	Course Type	Number of Sisters
Master's Degree	Public Administration	01
Bachelor's Degree	Education/Teaching	01
	Accountant	01
Diploma	Human Resource Management	01
Certificate	Nursing	01
	Child Care Education	01
Secondary School	Sec. Education	04

Source: The report (2012) of education development of deaconesses.

The above tables show how deaconesses are empowered educationally in different levels and professions. Because they are empowered in their professions, they can become competent and efficient in their work. This may increase their morale and motivation for working. It appears that the educational empowerment and skills provided to deaconesses at Ushirika wa Neema enable them to promote positive changes in the community. For example, the provision of the counselling moulds the behaviour of the students and helps them to improve their learning as they conduct group discussion and other learning activities in a peaceful manner.

Also, the data show that Deaconesses equip children with the word of God through Biblical stories hence developing their faith. They teach boys and girls from a young age on how to respect each other and that all are equal as children of God. This is a valuable contribution to promote gender equality in the church and society. As Bible says in Proverb 22:6 "train up a child in a way he should go, and when he is old he will not depart from it". This shows that women empowerment may affect society to a larger extent. This agrees with the proverbs which says to educate a woman is to educate the whole nation and liberate the entire society.

Increase in Self-Confidence of Deaconesses

There is a perception that the education offered at UWN motivated deaconesses to perform their duties with confidence and happiness. Deaconesses shared a lot of positive comments which they observed when they were teaching kindergarten and Christian education in both primary and secondary schools. Deaconess 5 said: *"I use my skills which I acquired in ethics, guidance and counselling to provide counselling among students. This has changed the behaviours of the students to larger extent. They respect teachers and maintain a harmonious relationship within themselves. This situation provides a conducive environment for learning and teaching, hence improving students' performance."*

Deaconess 8 said: *"In kindergarten, I use my child psychology and skills I learned at Montessori College to interact with children. By doing so, I teach them Christian songs, the Ten Commandments, short stories in the Bible, counting and how to write. I teach them that boys and girls are all equal and they are all children of God. When they join primary school, they already know how to read and write."*

EMPOWERMENT AND AUTONOMY OF WOMEN

The above quotations indicate that educational empowerment offered at Ushirika wa Neema seemed to empower female teachers and enable them to be competent in their professions.

Empowerment of Deaconesses Leadership

Ushirika wa Neema Deaconess Centre contributes to the empowerment of women by enabling deaconesses to potentially hold administrative positions in different sectors in the ELCT-Northern Diocese. Deaconess 2 clarified this by mentioning that a few posts which are held by deaconesses were traditionally held by men in many societies for many years. She points out: "*Agape Lutheran Junior Seminary is led by Deaconess Elistaha Mlay. Lyamungo Retreat Centre is led by Deaconess Rev. Elly Urio. Lutheran Uhuru Hotel is also led by deaconesses. Other deaconesses are matrons in schools, nurses and clinical officers in church hospitals. They are very creative, cooperative and committed to fulfilling their responsibilities faithfully.*"

Moreover, deaconesses are empowered to be leaders through education and training in different professions. Aaron Urioh said: "*For Deaconess Sisters to be leaders, we empower them through education. By doing so, they qualify for different posts in the church and community. For example, we have supported Deaconess Sister Flaviana Temba until she earned a Master's Degree in Accounting. Currently, she is a treasurer of Lutheran Mission Cooperation (LMC) Tanzania, a position which was held by men for long time.*"

During the interviews, the deaconess leaders of different institutions were asked: how do they lead in patriarchal oriented institutions? They argued that they are well empowered to use a collaborative leadership style in their organizations. Deaconess 3 said:

> *I usually solve school problems by working with my fellow school leaders. If a problem becomes very difficult to solve, I arrange a committee meeting to look at the problem. I never force anybody to do something. I use a dialogue to make a decision. I don't make the decision alone. If we*

> *are introducing a new system or policy in school, I make sure all schools' stakeholders are involved, that is teachers, student representatives and parent representatives. This makes people feel that the decisions are their own and therefore they are motivated to implement it. By doing so we have built more teachers' houses, increased students' hostels and classes, fenced the school's compound. We have managed to drill for some water and supply water in the school compounds.*

The above information indicates that there is a perception that education has contributed to the deaconess' ability to qualify to understand different institutions in the ELCT-Northern diocese. They have the potential to be better leaders than men. Also, it seems that deaconess leaders practice participatory leadership, which includes collaboration and teamwork rather than hierarchical structures and authority. This to some extent motivates performance in the contemporary world. This view agrees with some researchers who have reported that women are very good leaders and administrators due to the fact that they learn from their childhood stages about how to handle different issues in everyday life.[48] According to Blyth and Robins[49] women leaders tend to be collaborative, inclusive and more attentive to things like process and dialogue. This can extend the decision-making process and can generate ownership, understanding and support. They are very responsible and sensitive to other people's problems. On the other hand, some studies have also reported that there is a socialization and cultural influence in the perception of women's leadership qualification and effectiveness. Dr. Chandler (2011) in her article '*What women bring to the exercise of leadership*' points out that gender prejudice aligns with social constructions of masculine and feminine based on cultural perception and influences. According to her women leaders are associated with communal

---

48. King, *Feminist Theology from Third World*, 5–15.
49. Blyth, M. & Robison, *No Boundaries to Compassion?*, 26.

qualities of compassion, affection, gentleness and men associated with qualities of self-confidence and dominance.⁵⁰

Challenges facing Deaconesses in Chagga Patriarchal Society

The study also explored the challenges which deaconesses face in their diaconal ministry in the Chagga patriarchal society. During the interview sessions, deaconesses were asked a question: what are the cultural, social and economic challenges which you face in your service? Deaconesses shared some challenges which they are facing in their services.

Marriage, Celibacy and Cultural Challenges

The majority of deaconesses said that they face a challenge of indirect stigmatization from the Chagga patriarchal society because they have not married. For example deaconesses 10 and 7 argue: *"Among the challenge which we are facing is the Chagga value of marriage. Marriage and bearing of children is considered as the means of maintenance and empowering a generation. Unmarried women like us in the Chagga ethnic group are seen as women who escape marriage responsibilities in the family."*

In the same vein, Deaconesses 9 said: *Some people view us as those ladies who do not want to bear children. Some people discourage my parents when I was joining the nunnery by telling them you would not get grandchildren from me. Thus my parents were reluctant to allow me to join deaconess sisterhood."* This view is consistent with the Mother of deaconesses who shares her experiences by saying:

> When I was joining the deaconess ministry in the 1980s, I was discouraged by one male pastor who was a district pastor. He criticized the deaconess sisters and their celibate life. He told my parents, 'Is your daughter barren? If you

---

50. Chandler, *What Women bring to the Exercise of Leadership* 68.

> *allow her to join Ushirika wa Neema –Deaconess Centre, you will not get grandchildren from her." This upset my parents so much, but I kept on praying and convincing my parents to permit me to join the deaconess ministry because I felt called by God. Pastor Aaron Urio talked with my parents until they understood and allowed me to join the celibate life so that I could devote my life totally to serve the Lord.*

Some of the young deaconesses confess to facing the problem that some people look down upon them because they have decided to live the celibate life, and some boys are still approaching them for marriage and this puts them in a dilemma. Deaconess 9 points out that:

> *My neighbour in my village looks down upon me, telling me, 'Why does a beautiful girl like you agree to live a celibate life? Leave it so that you may marry our son. If it is a matter of serving the Lord, you will serve Him even if you get married.' This boy I schooled with in primary school also started to approach me for marriage. He disturbed me greatly via my mobile phone. You know I am a human being with emotions and desires like other human beings. This issue is putting me into dilemma. But I have taken the vow of sisterhood and committed my life to Christ. I pray that God can help me to keep my vow for life.*

Similarly, the chaplain, argued that some of the deaconesses left the deaconess ministry and got married because of the family pressures and desires of the world. He further said:

> *Some girls who are in a probation period of becoming deaconesses, particularly from the Maasai tribe, are forced by their parents and relatives to marry. Some of them have left the deaconess training and got married. We cannot stop them. They have the freedom to make that choice. However, culture is very powerful. For example one pastor in the Maasai area was beaten so much to the extent of being admitted to the hospital because he forbid his congregants to practice female genital mutilation and arranged a plan which made Maasai boys in his church to be circumcised*

> in the hospital. *They took them and did their rituals and re-circumcised them. The Masaai parents take the bride price of their girls without the consent of their daughters. They just come and take them to husbands.*

The above quotes indicate that both old and young deaconesses are facing cultural challenges from the community. There some people who do not understand the deaconess sisterhood ministry. This is why they look down upon women who decided to live the celibate life. A lack of knowledge of the deaconess sisterhood fosters tension between traditional cultural values and Christian beliefs. The issue here is the tension between African cultural values and the model of deaconess which based on celibate life which seems to be a new phenomenon in the ELCT-Northern Diocese countering traditional norm of marriage and bearing of children. In line with this argument, Mbiti comments on the importance of marriage by saying that: "Marriage fulfils the obligation, the duty and the custom that every normal person should be married and bear children . . . failure to get married is like committing a crime against traditional beliefs and practices . . . The supreme purpose of marriage according to African people is to bear children, to build a family, to extend life, and to hand down the living torch of human existence."[51]

This quotation implies that marriage in many African societies is like an institution which is useful for extending life to the next generation. This view is in agreement with Mbiti who further discusses the importance of bearing a child by saying: "The arrival of a child in the family is one of the greatest blessings of life . . . If it is the first pregnancy for her (a woman), it assures everyone that she is able to bear children. Once that is known, her marriage is largely secure and the relatives treat her with greater respect than before."[52]

The above quotation portrays the culture of Chagga tribe whereby marriage and bearing of the children is respected and considered as a way of continuing life from one generation to

---

51. Mbiti, *Introduction to African Traditional Religion*, 104–105.
52. Ibid, 75.

The Empowerment of Women by *Ushirika wa Neema*

another generation. Wachagga believe that God enables husband and wife to start a life.[53] They use a phase *Ruwa Molunga Soka na Mndo* which means: the being that is capable of joining an axe and sickle. This Chagga proverb means that God unites male and female through marriage and gives them blessings of children. Therefore, a girl, who refuses to engage in marriage, contradicts with Chagga culture as stated above and she appears not to want to extend the life to the next generation. As Mbiti pointed out that failure to get married is like committing a crime against traditional beliefs and practices.[54] However, the deaconesses are allowed to leave the community if they get married or find that the deaconessate was not their calling. According to their rules, once a deaconess got married she cannot continue with her deaconess ministry.

I was interested to know if Ushirika wa Neema Deaconess Centre has any plan to help those deaconesses who drop out of their vocation. Aaron Urioh said:

> *We have a plan to establish a new deaconess centre which will enrol women whose ages are from 35 years to 65 years. Women in this new centre will not stay together with our deaconess sisters at Ushirika wa Neema. This will be a special centre for deaconesses like widows, single mothers, and married women, sisters who decided to bear a child, or got married, aged women who are not married and want to offer their life to serve God. They will have their own Mother and Chaplain. We have got a place and buildings at Karanga in Moshi. The name of this centre has also been approved which is the Dorcas Community.*

Ushirika wa Neema seems to consider positively the women who want to be deaconess without practicing celibate life and the deaconess sisters who want to be married by establishing a new centre for them. This approach will increase the chance of women to participate in the church services. Also, it will be an alternative for those deaconesses who decide to marry. They will continue to serve the community and church as a married deaconess without

---

53. Shao, *Bruno Gutman's Missionary Method*, 42.
54. Mbiti, *Introduction to African Traditional Religion*, 75.

feeling the guilt of marrying. Also it will eliminate a stigma from both society and church and enable the married deaconesses to carry out their social and spiritual roles comfortably.

Leadership and Gender Challenges

Some of the old deaconesses who are leaders shared the difficult experiences which they faced as the leaders in institutions which are male dominated, particularly those situated in the villages. Deaconess 2 argues that: "*I faced a lot of challenges in my leadership because of the cultural belief that leaders are men. I worked hard to convince men in my school and surrounding communities that I am capable of leading like men. I used a lot of efforts in the beginning in parents' meetings to show them that I will run the schools effectively to achieve school goals like men.*"

In line with this argument informant 6 said: "*Young boys from initiation practices tend to come with negative attitudes towards women. It takes us time to discipline them.*" This attitude implies that the deaconess leaders are facing a difficulty in being accepted as leaders in Chagga patriarchal society. They work hard to convince the community that they can do better in leadership like men whereas men are easily accepted even if they are not competent.

Therefore, cultural stereotypes and prejudices against women make it difficult for women leaders to utilize the talents and leadership potential which God has bestowed on them. Women leaders should not be neglected because of gender, but society should give them collaboration and cooperation as they do for men so that they may fulfil their leadership responsibilities well. In rural areas where patriarchal cultures are still active, there is a need for the church to continue teaching people to respect women leaders and erase the cultural concepts that women are not leaders but are just custodians of the family. They should be helped to identify the contribution of women leaders in the society. In this scenario, Oduyoye[55] makes it clear that women alone cannot

---

55. Oduyoye M. *Who Will Roll the Stone Away?* 23–40.

The Empowerment of Women by *Ushirika wa Neema*

eliminate gender injustices in the church and community. She calls church leaders in patriarchal society to collaborate and co-operate with women to eliminate oppressive practices which undermine women. By doing so the church will be a place where both men and women serve the Lord with equal respect and mutual understanding. On the other hand, as we have seen in chapter five that Oduyoye cautioned that this collaboration should be done in a way which does not let women be assimilated to the existing structures of dominance, patriarchy and hierarchy in the church and society. She insists that in order for this collaboration of women and men to be sustainable in the church, there should be an establishment of partnerships and the sharing of ecclesial responsibilities.

Kurubai reported that in many dioceses and societies in Tanzania they still have the perception that men are the ones who can rule the community and consequently women are neglected and placed under men and face the following disadvantages:

1. Women's role tend to be pushed into invisibility and anonymity
2. They are not included in decision making but they are expected to comply with the decisions being made and to assist in their implementation.[56]

Similarly, Karl states: "Women are poorly represented in the ranks of power, policy and decision-making. Women are found in large numbers in low-level positions of public administrations.[57] This view agrees with Fiorenza who state that governing boards and decision- making positions are often restricted to male clergy.[58] Women clergy who have qualifications to be leaders are not given opportunity to exercise their leadership; instead they are given secondary status and remain at the level of assistant ministers. Also, Oduyoye and Kanyoro reported that African patriarchal culture

---

56. Kurubai, R. M. *From Doubt to Acceptance*, 59.
57. Karl, *Women and Empowerment*, 6.
58. Fiorenza, *Waiting-at-Table*, 83.

has been used to dominate women.[59] Furthermore, Oduyoye observed that in any relationship within which African women engage, they are placed at lower level due to the hierarchies of patriarchy.[60] This has undermined African women and caused them to lack autonomy. Their identity is completely constructed in relation to men.

Taking a close look and observing the leadership structure of the ELCT I noticed that it is still patriarchally-oriented because among top officers of the dioceses and among the district Pastors there is few women as leaders. This may be taken as indicating that the church has not helped the women church members enough in acquiring and demonstrating their leadership potential. Maybe the church has embraced the patriarchal customs and practices that the Chagga people have against women being leaders, as originated from '*Mangi system*'. Mangi was a title for male Chagga rulers. In that system, majority of the women were not allowed to become *Mangis*. The Chaggas have a traditional saying which states that "*Mka chi msongorupho, moka kanyi na msoro nyi msongoru na mosaura*" which literally means "*women are not rulers, they are custodians of the family and men are rulers and seekers of the needs of families.*"

Furthermore, Mwaura argues that "in Africa women form 80% of believers, yet are usually absent from its decision-making bodies."[61] Furthermore, the WCC Report on the result of mid Ecumenical Decade of Churches in Solidarity with Women (1994–1996) observes that women all over the world are the pillars of the church and majority in most congregations. They are active, participating strongly in the spiritual and liturgical life of the church's mission. But many churches have failed to receive and respond fully to women's gifts and have failed to admit them into the key areas of participation such as leadership. Thus women have not been reflected in leadership positions and high level of decision-making and governance whether in the church or society. For example, as

59. Kanyoro, *Introducing Feminist Cultural Hermeneutics*, 23.
60. Oduyoye, *Who Will Roll the Stone Away?*, 23–40.
61. Mwaura, *Empowerment of Women*, 32.

The Empowerment of Women by *Ushirika wa Neema*

we note in chapter two, in the Executive Council of the Church, which is the next highest decision- making body to the General Assembly of ELCT, amongst its fifty two members only five are women who do not reflect their membership and contribution to the general growth of the church. In other decision-making organs of the ELCT such as church councils in the district and parishes, women constitute less than 20%.[62] Similarly, Karl states:

> Women are poorly represented in the ranks of power, policy and decision-making. Women make up less than 5 per cent of the world's head of State, head of Major Corporation and top positions in international organizations. Women are not just behind in political and managerial equity, they are a long way behind. This is in spite of the fact that women are found in large numbers in low-level positions of public administrations, political parties, trade union and business.[63]

This implies that in patriarchal society women are given secondary status and those few female leaders find various challenges in their ministries because of the patriarchal practices which undermine women and exclude them in leadership and decision-making positions. This is practiced in Chagga patriarchal society and other parts of Tanzania. This agrees with Rhoda who observed that many decisions in Tanzania, including decisions about women's own lives, are made by men.[64] Similarly Phiri argues that oppressive cultural practices especially patriarchy are major setbacks which hinder women to be leaders in the church and society.[65] Thus, because of gender inequality in the patriarchal church women have been given auxiliary roles and secondary status in the ministry, and have not been involved in decision-making.[66]

In my view, one facet that could hamper the process of women empowerment is Chagga patriarchal ideology of masculinity,

---

62. www.elct.org/social.html. Retrieved on 28.10.2011.
63. Karl, *Women and Empowerment*, 6.
64. Rhoda, *Prostitution, Culture And Church*, 11.
65. Phiri, *Doing Theology* (1997).
66. Fiorenza, *Waiting-at-Table*, 84–89.

which places women under men and makes women into second-class citizens. Some women have, to some extent, internalized this ideology. In this scenario, men are socialized into a superior class and express masculine roles of self-assertion, independence and control, whereas women are viewed as inferior to, and controlled by, men. This situation questions the kind of empowerment needed to liberate women from that masculine ideology. I find this attitude very oppressive to women, because it implies and allows violence towards women, especially when church leaders and clan leaders use romantic language, saying that women should obey their husbands in order to keep peace in the home. Even if a husband has made a mistake, women are told to ask for forgiveness. It is very important to provide gender training and awareness to both men and women, in order to change gradually this masculine ideology and promote gender complementarity. The idea of gender complementarity is based on the understanding of men and women being biologically and essentially different, and that these differences are constitutional to their social roles, responsibilities and tasks. At the same time these differences are seen complementary. In their differences, men and women complement each other and form a composite whole.[67]

Moreover, Oduyoye insists that the church should support fairness in representation of women in various church bodies. Also the church should encourage participation of women in decision-making. She further insists that the church is made up of both men and women. Women should be included in leadership positions as partner ministers in the church. Therefore, men and women need to learn and appreciate the role played by each other in order to bring a full communion within the body of Christ.[68]

---

67. Tønnessen, *gender complemetarity*, 63.
68. Oduyoye, *Who Will Roll the Stone Away?* 23–40.

The Empowerment of Women by *Ushirika wa Neema*

Financial Challenges

The financial system at Ushirika wa Neema was mentioned as a challenge by some deaconesses. Deaconess 2 said that: "*They are facing personal financial challenges because they are not paid. Their salaries are paid to the deaconess centre. They don't have access to their salaries. If they have any problem they must ask from their leaders. They claim that they cannot help their parents and relatives to do things which need lot of money because their pocket money is very limited.*" This statement is in line with Deaconess 4 who said: "*I come from a peasant family. My parents still live in a mud house. If I was paid my full salary, I could build a modern house with bricks for my parents. Also I could take my young brother to private secondary school. But I can't do all these because of the system of our communal life. Like apostles we work and put our incomes together and share it together.*"

The Chaplain and Mother of deaconesses had differing opinions. The Chaplain said:

Deaconess Sisters are very committed to working hard because they know they are not working for somebody. Rather they are working for their communal life and benefits. No one exploits their income. They bring their income together and share it together like the apostles in the early church." Whereas the Mother of deaconesses insisted that: "*This togetherness is the foundation of our new family as deaconess sisters. The main challenge is how to make sisters to feel at home in this new family. If a sister has a problem like the death of a relative, we give her some money to handle the situation. Also, once one has happy events like a wedding, we also support through buying a gift and giving her some money so that she may attend.*"

This aspect is in agreement with three older deaconesses who argue that: "*Before joining the deaconess sisterhood during the interview, they are informed that they are going to start a new life for Christ. They will live a communal life and all of their income will be collected in one basket and shared together. Since they have a call and are informed, this is the life they choose to live for Christ.*"

Empowerment and Autonomy of Women

It seems that there is a dilemma between deaconess and their leaders on issues of income. Also, the older deaconesses have a different understanding of such issues compared to the younger deaconesses. Old deaconesses to large extent adhere to the principles of communal life at Ushirika wa Neema, but some young deaconesses Sisters have critical challenges on their salaries. They seem to have some ambitions such as to build houses for their parents, to assist their relatives to acquire secondary education but they are facing the barrier of income. This situation led to questioning the system of one basket for all. In this case, one deaconess said: "*Deacons are paid 70% of their salaries. Only 30% is paid to their centre. This policy should also apply to us.*" It seems as if some deaconesses wish for such policy to be applied to them too, so that they may be able to provide more help to their parents and family. Here, two things are important to consider, the first is deacon is married and has children. They live with their families and do not live in one centre like the deaconess sisters, even though they have a schedule to meet every month. This makes a big difference when compared with sisters who are not married and living in the nunnery. The second thing to consider is that some of deaconesses come from a poor peasant family background means that they have financial constraints. This view is in line with Chaplain who said: "*The minority of deaconess applicants comes from families where parents or guardians worked in professional employment like teachers, clergy, accountants, bankers. The majority of them usually come from peasant families and have little formal education.*" Deaconess Sisters from such background are compelled to assist their parents and relatives in order to liberate them from poverty.

High Demands vs the Capacity of Providing Help

Some deaconesses said that they are facing the challenge of helping large numbers of needy people in the society compared to the ability of Ushirika wa Neema. Six deaconesses made a similar point: "*Epidemic diseases like HIV/AIDS kill many people and increase the number of orphans, widows, widowers and elderly people who suffer from multiple problems. This brings a challenge to our centre on how to serve people who need both spiritual and physical help from us."* In the same vein Deaconess 9 said:

> Many orphans need help and protection after the death of the parents. They need care and love. After the death of their parents, children remain alone or with their grandparents who are not able to help them. Most of the relatives do not care for the orphans. The majority of them used to come to our centre to ask for help. We don't have the ability to help all of them. For example our centre at Kalali can accommodate only a few orphans. But the demand is so much higher than our capacity that I find it a challenge in our ministry to church and society.

Similarly, Deaconess 8 Said:

> In the provision of our diaconal ministry in society, we find some challenges such as children who lose their parents, and widows who lose their husbands. There is a tendency to lose their rights, i.e. loss of property, e.g. shelter, material goods inherited land, livestock and agricultural goods. In most cases the remaining relatives tend to take and misuse their property. We find it very challenging to handle such issues which are not reported to the police. In reality widows and orphans need to be empowered so that they can live a standard life like other people in the society.

According to the information from the above informants, it appears that the number of orphans and widows increase rapidly as an impact of HIV/AIDS. Mmbando et al, reported that in Tanzania there were 1 million children without parents due to HIV/AIDS. Among that number 40,000 are infected with HIV. Even though there is NGOs and community-based organization to help these children, still many orphans are not attended.[69] Orphans and widows are not only caused by HIV/AIDS but can be attributed by other diseases, accidents and calamities.

Furthermore, the deaconesses' information shows that most of the time orphans and widows are marginalized and oppressed

---

69. Mmbando et al, *Care for the most vulnerable children*, 13–20.

by their relatives in their extended families. There is a need to inform them about laws which help to protect them, such as child labour laws and amended inheritance laws. Even the Bible insists that orphans and widows should be protected and their advantages should not be taken away from them. Exodus 22: 22–24 *"do not take advantage of a widow or an orphan. If you do and they cry out to me, I will certainly hear their cry. My anger will be aroused, and I will kill you with the sword; your wives will become widows and your children fatherless."* There is a need to protect the orphans and widows. This is crucial due to the fact that these are two groups of people who are at high risk of losing their inheritance rights of the property of their parents or husbands if they are not well protected.

Conclusion

This chapter has shown that UWN contributes to the empowerment of women in the church and society in different ways, such as providing important skills and techniques of life, like gardening, animal keeping, cooking varieties of food and establishing women entrepreneurs. Also, UWN contributes to empower women to access independent income through self-employment which helps them to improve their standard of living in society and raise their status and respect in society and increase the chance of women to participate more in the decision-making process. The centre also trains women to be Montessori kindergarten teachers and conducts women's seminars which raise gender awareness in society. Also, the chapter shows that deaconesses are empowered through education which increases their self-confidence and efficiency in their work. They are also enabled to be leaders in different institutions. On the other hand, the chapter points out that deaconesses confront a challenge of stigmatization from the Chagga patriarchal society because they have not married. Other challenges were financial constraints and women leadership and gender challenges. The next chapter presents the conclusion.

CHAPTER 7

Summary, Conclusion, and Recommendations

Introduction

THIS CHAPTER OFFERS A conclusion to the book. It is divided into three sections. The first section presents the summary of the book. The second section is a conclusion. Lastly, it presents some recommendations for improvement and for further research in the area related to this book.

Summary of the Study

The main objective of this book was to examine how Ushirika wa Neema Centre empowers women in the ELCT-Northern Diocese, fostering gender awareness in the church and society and to analyze the challenges which deaconesses at Ushirika wa Neema are facing in Chagga patriarchal society.

The motivation for writing this book has grown out of an interest to learn how deaconesses empower women in Chagga society, which contributes in influencing gender awareness in both church and society. Moreover, this interest was strengthened after my preaching at Ushirika wa Neema deaconess chapel in 2010. After the sermon, I was shown various projects and services conducted by deaconess sisters. I was informed how different women's groups visit the centre in order to learn important skills for life. Since then, I developed a desire to explore their activities from the perspective of gender and to carry out the research so that I could describe how they are contributing to the empowerment of women and identify the challenges facing them in the Chagga patriarchal society.

This book was limited to Ushirika wa Neema deaconess centre in the Evangelical Lutheran Church in Tanzania –Northern Diocese in Kilimanjaro, specifically Moshi. It involved soliciting the views of deaconesses, bishops, pastors, Montessori kindergarten teachers and women. The book encountered some limitations, one of which was the lack of written sources regarding the contribution of the centre to the empowerment of women and history of the deaconess ministry in ELCT-Northern Diocese.

The literature reviewed identified different roles of deaconesses in the church and society. Empirical studies revealed that women are still relegated to inferior status in economic, political, social, intellectual and religious spheres. Their numbers have not been reflected in leadership positions or at high level of decision-making processes and governance, whether in church or society. Many decisions in Tanzania, including decisions about women's own lives, are made by men. Patriarchal societies maintain gender hierarchy, male supremacy and subordinate women to men. Because of gender inequality in the patriarchal church, women have been given auxiliary roles and secondary status in the ministry.

The conceptual frameworks applied in the study were feminist and empowerment theories. Feminist theories are divided into three waves named first wave, second wave and third wave. The focus of the study was on Third-Wave feminism which is a feminist movement that began in the 1990s up to the present. It involves the economic, political, social, and personal empowerment of women. Also, it focuses more on the individual empowerment of women than on activism. It promotes women to build meaningful identities in the complex contemporary world. In this scenario, empowerment is used enables women to have control over their lives and make their own decision. The study discussed various aspects of empowerment such as female educational empowerment and economic empowerment. Women educational empowerment is among the factors which promotes gender mainstreaming in the society. This is because education is one among the significant means of empowering women with the knowledge, skills and self-confidence which are essential to participate fully in the development process. This study has claimed that education helps girls and women to know their rights and to gain confidence to claim them. It also reveals that economic empowerment enables women to set up businesses and projects.

This study avers that the learning of different skills at Ushirika wa Neema make women more independent and self-reliant. Ushirika wa Neema has had a crucial role in developing alternative ways for women who want to be independent from a patriarchal system and to generate income. This has helped women, to some extent, to emerge from their traditional roles, and it is apparent that women are now more knowledgeable about the mobilization, allocation and control of resources. This is due to the fact that such business opportunities empower them to influence decisions in their families and the community. This also increases their confidence and self-esteem. The study noted that empowerment was used as a way of increasing the well-being, societal development, and focus on self-sufficiency which aimed at addressing the practical needs of women instead of changing power relations between men and women in the church and community.

The book employed a qualitative research method. Semi-structured interviews were used to collect data. Oral interviews with deaconesses, bishops, pastors, Montessori kindergarten teachers and women were conducted face to face. In addition, written sources were read.

Conclusion

On the basis of this book, Ushirika wa Neema seemed to play a great role to empower women through provision of important skills and techniques of life such as gardening, animal keeping, cooking varieties of food and the establishment of women entrepreneurs. This seems an important way for the deaconesses to increase the empowerment of women in the church and society. The learning of different skills makes them more independent, self-reliant and increases their confidence, self-esteem and empowers them to influence decisions in their families and the community.

The training offered by deaconesses to women's groups contributes to the creation of employment opportunities for women in the informal sector. As a result, that informal sector becomes a very important source of employment for women in Tanzania. Thus some of the women seemed to engage in small businesses and have access to income and credit. It was noted that women empowerment and employment is changing gender relations at the household level and can lead to women being viewed as important partners in life, since their economic contribution is felt at both household and public level.

The skills acquired by women groups in terms of running small projects, seemed to empower single mothers and women in society to build houses, pay school fees and for health services and raise fund for church activities. It has also been noted that the respect for women and agency increased within the household as well as outside, due to the changes which happened on a personal level. The training acquired by women from Ushirika wa Neema increases their status, as some of them were consulted to give advice in their families and community more than before. This book acknowledges that women's decision making regarding financial issues, children's schooling, running businesses and family matters, had increased compared to the situation before they acquired training and skills from Ushirika wa Neema. This was a result of the independent income generated from small businesses and projects.

Moreover, Ushirika wa Neema provides women with opportunities to acquire Montessori kindergarten education and careers which seem to promote women empowerment in the church and society. Women and girls who undertake the training offered at Ushirika wa Neema Deaconess Centre participate more in the

Summary, Conclusion, and Recommendations

labour force and are employed in different kinds of jobs in church and private institutions. Women who have good employment opportunities are mostly financially stable and do not have to depend on their husbands all the time. Also, their chance to contribute to the household needs increases, a role that was traditionally left to men in many societies.

Even though the book shows that there is some changes in decision-making after the engagement of women in economic projects offered at Ushirika wa Neema, domestic activities have remained unchanged to majority of women. Men who assist their wives in performing house activities are still minimal, and those who try to do that are discouraged by their friends and relatives. This indicates that there had not been a big change of men towards women's roles. To a large extent, most women often participate in the economic activities at the same time performing the domestic activities. In patriarchal society women's housework contribution is not recognized in the formal economic activities and is not regarded as important in the realm of economic growth and development.

The education and seminars conducted by Ushirika wa Neema seem to contribute toward empowering women from different parishes all over Tanzania. These help women to respond to their contemporary challenges in a patriarchal society, such as to challenge oppressive structures in church and community. Also, the knowledge which women acquired in the seminars at Ushirika wa Neema seems be a tool for awakening their conscietization and consciousness, which are the fundamental factors in influencing gender awareness and empowerment of women in the society and church.

Deaconesses are empowered, through education and training, to be leaders in different professions in the church and community based institutions. The deaconess leaders practice participatory leadership, which includes collaboration and teamwork. This deaconess leadership contributes to change the mindset of the patriarchal society, proving that women can be better leaders.

This book indicated that both older and younger deaconesses are facing cultural challenges from the Chagga patriarchal community. There is tension between Chagga cultural values and the celibate life style of the deaconesses at Ushirika wa Neema, which directly counters Chagga traditional social values of marriage and child bearing. Deaconess leaders in Chagga patriarchal society, and particularly those who are working in the villages, face some challenges because of the patriarchal belief that women are not leaders. Sometimes male workers do not support them effectively. They don't want to receive orders and instructions from deaconess leaders. However, deaconesses and women are still practicing their leadership at low levels in church institutions.

Recommendations

On the basis of the findings of my book, the following are recommended:

First, in rural areas, where patriarchal cultures are still active, there is a need for the church to continue teaching people to accommodate deaconess and women leaders within their social structure and change the cultural concept that women are not leaders but are just custodians of the family. They should be helped to recognize the potential contribution of women leaders in their society.

Second, given that patriarchy often makes it difficult for women to be elected as Bishops or assistant Bishops, this study recommends that gender should be taken into account. In correcting past gender imbalances, the focus should be on attaining gender parity by integrating women into the leading posts within the church administrative structures.

Third, the ELCT-Northern Diocese institutions, NGOs and governmental bodies should increase the effort to promote empowerment of women. Strategies and mechanism for gender equality must be strengthened. Church policy makers and governmental policy makers should formulate policies which promote gender equality.

Fourth, this study suggests that there is a need to put in practice those policies which promote gender equality in the church and society.

Fifth, there is a need to provide more education of a deaconess sisterhood which practices a celibate life style in order to tackle the tension between Chagga cultural values of marriage and celibate life.

Recommendations for Further Studies

Since the book dealt with the contribution of Ushirika wa Neema to the empowerment of women in the Evangelical Lutheran Church in Tanzania—Northern Diocese and cultural challenges, there is a need to conduct further research on the impact of skills acquired by women from Ushirika wa Neema of establishing small projects and businesses.

APPENDIX 1

History of the Evangelical Lutheran Church in Tanzania

THE LUTHERAN CHURCH BEGAN its activities in the country during the 19th Century. It has continued to bear fruit despite interruptions by the Hehe/German War in 1891, the Majimaji war of 1905–1906, the 1st World War 1914–1918 and later on the 2nd World War of 1939–1945. By 1938 there were seven Churches in Tanganyika, as the country was known at that time. These were: The Lutheran Church of Northern Tanganyika in the north, the Usambara/Digo Lutheran Church in the northeast, the Uzaramo/Uluguru Lutheran Church in the east, the Augustana Lutheran Church of Irimba/Turu located in Central Tanganyika, the Evangelical Lutheran Church in the North West Tanganyika, the Iraqw Lutheran Church in the Northern Province, and the Ubena/Konde Lutheran Church in the Southern Highlands. In 1938, the Churches founded a federation known as the Federation of Lutheran Churches in Tanganyika, which brought together these seven churches. On June 19, 1963, the seven Churches, under the umbrella of a federation, merged to become a single Church, known as the Evangelical Lutheran Church in Tanzania[1]. The membership of the ELCT increase yearly; for example, in January 2012 was 5,825,312 compared to 5601,271 members in 2010,

1. Online at http://www.elct.org/# Retrieved on 19/09/2015

APPENDIX 1

having registered 224,041 new members. The Secretary General of the ELCT, Mr. Brighton Kilewa, shows an increase of 4 per cent from the previous year. The figures for the past five years are as follows: in 2007 there were 4,632,480 members, 2008 (4,956,731 members), 2009 (5,303,727 members), 2010 (5,601,217 members) and in January 2011 there were 5,825,312 members.[2]

---

2. Online at http://www.elct.org/news/2012.05.001.html. Retrieved on 19/09/2012.

APPENDIX 2

Testimony of the First Missionaries at *Ushirika wa Neema*

SR. HOFMANN AND SR. Gisela were the first missionaries who worked as pioneers in establishing the deaconess ministry in Northern Diocese (Ushirika wa Neema). In her letter dated 25.10.2012, Sr Hofman had the following to say as her testimony:

> In my entire life I have never thought of migrating from the land where I was born. Even though, I occasionally read about the missionaries who travelled overseas, I preferred staying closer to my mother country home. In 1978 I worked as a social worker in the post of a Deacon in Nurnberg, Bavaria, where I was sent by Evang. Diakonissenaanstalt Augsburg, our Motherhouse. October 1978 I went to Augsburg, for the Bible study week so as to find new strength in my ministry. A day after reaching there I was called in by our Rector Steghoefer, where he told me that the motherhouse has got a request of sending two sisters to Tanzania with a mission of helping start up and establish a sister's Coventry in the northern part of Tanzania. One of our sisters, Sister Gisela Kausch had already offered herself to be sent and she was looking for a partner to accompany her.
>
> I was overwhelmed with gratitude and fear, I didn't know how to respond, but I gathered enough courage and asked when they required my response: I was given a week

to respond with an answer. My mind was running fast as I thought of the stories about the missionaries who went on mission overseas, how some of them died, how others took so long in coming back home and only returning in their old age; I feared that I would become a victim of the same fate. I wondered will I get to see my brothers after being sent there. I knew the only one who can grant me the answers I needed was God; without talking to anyone I went straight to our church to seek the divine intervention I so needed. God never disappointed me as through his word I found the answers I needed. His word in the book of Luke 1:46–48 filled me with joy and gratitude rather than worries. I was so encouraged and felt like I was ready for the journey. The only thing that was left was to talk to my father who was all alone after my mother's death, but to my surprise my father received the news positively where he said that it was a call from God for me to go on that mission. Since this was a big and a new venture that motherhouse was investing in, Rector Steghoefer and Sr. Lise Lotte Sperl felt that it was wise to perform a thorough analysis of the project before investing in it. They suggested we visit the site where the sisters house was to be built and conduct a viability analysis and the requirement analysis of building the Coventry there. Therefore the architect Schatzs, motherhouse board chairman and I took a trip to Moshi on 31st March 1979 where we spent two weeks. We were warmly welcomed to Moshi by Bishop Erasto Kweka, general secretary Shadrack Ngowi, Mother Veronica Swai, the department of women and others. For the two weeks that we stayed there, Mother Swai took us through a tour of different projects organized and supported by women groups, among them was different girl's high schools and young men self help projects. From the trip, it was noted that women are playing a very big role in the development of the community and the country at large. On our way back to Augsburg, our KLM flight passed over the magnificent Kilimanjaro Mountain, giving us a life time chance of seeing the famous Kibo crater. The awesome view of the mountain made us realize the might of our God above. On 28th July 1979, almost all the sisters from motherhouse gathered to bid us farewell. Our plane left Munich from

Testimony of the First Missionaries

Kilimanjaro Airport on 29th July 1979. On 19th August 1979, Rector Steghoefer, architect Schatz, Klaus Hofmann and Werner Ranzmeyer arrived in Tanzania and joined us in starting the project. Our first priority in a foreign country was to learn how to communicate with the natives effectively; therefore we enrolled for Kiswahili lessons at language school in Tanzania for a period of five months, from 29th July to 04th December 1979.

In December 1979, Sr.Gisela and I completed our languages classes and moved in to Uhuru-Hostel. The first meeting was held at Uhuru Hostel and from this meeting we realized that Ushirika wa Neema was the name that was picked for the new mission. A day later, all the members of the council, among them Bishop Erasto Kweka, Rector Steghoefer, Mr. Schatz, chairman Ngowi, Mr. Mshomi, Mr. Kamm and other members of the council from Germany, gathered at the site. We were also shown the place where the construction was to be done; the mango tree that had grown there was a clear indication that the ground was fertile for crop growing. The priest started the service and then Rector Steghoefer followed with a short sermon from the book of John; afterwards they mixed the first concrete in front of 30 witnesses to mark the commencement of the project. The construction started a day after the meeting, where the few contracted workers started by building a site house that was to be used as an office for the workers, a workshop, two main rooms for the workers, kitchen, store and a place where visitors can be hosted. The site house was completed and it was used for a period of nine years up to 1988 when the first house was completed.

Sr. Gisela, with the assistance of one of the workers, started a chicken rearing project; part of his work also included a construction of a thatched house. The thatched house was started in a bid to try and utilize the raw materials that were obtained from the land and tall grasses. On my part, I started a vegetable growing project with the help of Paul, one of the contracted workers. Andy Klause, Hoffman's wife, arrived and took part in house work. In addition, we designed labels that preached diaconal messages and advice to young girls.

Bibliography

Anuratha, K. P. Anuratha, *Gender Equality and Development*. New Delhi: Adhyayan Publishers and Distributors, 2010.

Armbruster, Heidi. *Feminist Theories and Anthropology*, http:lit.polylog.org/2/eah-en.htm. 2000.

Sultan, Maheen. *Mapping Women's Empowerment. Experiences from Bangladesh, India and Pakistan*. Bangladesh: Bangladesh University Press, 2010.

Bagachwa, Daniel. The Informal Sector under Adjustment in Tanzania. In L.A. Msambichaka et al (Ed.). *Beyond Structural Adjustment Programme in Tanzania, Success, Failure, and New Perspectives*. Economic Research Bureau. Dar es Salaam: University of Dar es Salaam Press. 1995.

Ballington, Silva. *Tanzania Gender Observer Mission Report*. Pretoria: Electoral Institute of Southern Africa, 2000.

Barry, Marie-Louise, Herman Steyn, and Alan Brent. "Selection of Renewable Energy Technologies for Africa: Eight case studies in Rwanda, Tanzania and Malawi." *Renewable energy* 36, no. 11 (2011): 45-52.

Bell, John. *Doing your Research Project*. 3rd edition. Buckingham-Philphia: Open University Press, 1990.

Bendera, Shane, Bennell, Paul, Godfrey Kanyenze, Emrode Kimambo, Sixtus Kiwia, Tichafa Mbiriyakura, Faustin Mukyanuzi. *Vocational Education and Training in Tanzania and Zimbabwe in the Context of Economic Reform*. Education Research Paper. Department for International Development, 96 Victoria Street, London SW1E 5JL, England, United Kingdom., 1999.

Bond, Johanna. *Women's Rights in Ghana, Uganda, and Tanzania*. Carollina: Academic Press, 2006.

Breidlind, Anders. *Education, Indigenous Knowledge, and Development in the Global South*. New York: Routledge, 2013.

Bryman, Alan. *Social research methods*. Second Edition. Oxford: Oxford University Press, 2004.

———. *Social research methods*. Third Edition. Oxford: Oxford University Press, 2008.

Bibliography

———. *Social research methods.* Fourth Edition. Oxford: Oxford University Press, 2012.

Bhalalusesa, Eustella, P. *Education For All Initiatives and the Barriers to Educating Girls and Young Women in Tanzania.* In *Journal of the School of Education.* 2011.

Blyth, Robinson,Wendy S. *No Boundaries to Compassion? An Exploration of Women Gender and Diakonia.* Geneva: WCC, 1988.

Bheemarasetty, Praveena Devi. *Women's empowerment: A Challenge* Available at SSRN:http://ssrn.com/abstract=19970087. Retrieved on 30.11.2012.

Coleman, Mat. *Leadership and Management in Education.* Oxford: University Press, 2005.

Chandler, Diane. What women bring to the exercise of leadership? *Journal of Strategic Leadership.* Vol. 3 Iss 2 pp.1-12. Regent University, 2011.

Chamshana, Rodah. *Prostitution, Culture and Church: A Study of Gender Inequality in Chalinze, Tanzania.* Master Thesis: University of Oslo. 2011.

Creswell, John. *Research Design: Qualitative and mixed methods approaches.* Thousand Oaks, Calif: Sage Publications, 2003.

Clifford, Anne. *Introducing Feminist Theology.* Maryknoll. NY: Obis Books, 2000.

Donnelly, Jack. *Universal Human Rights in Theory and Practice.* Ithaca: Cornell University Press, 2003.

Esposito, John. Introduction Women, Religion and empowerment In Haddad, Yvonne Yazbeck (Ed), *Daughter of Abraham: Feminist thought in Judaism Christianity and Islam.* 2001.

Ezer, Tamar. "Inheritance Law in Tanzania: The Impoverishment of Widows and Daughters". Online: *http://www.winafrica.org/.../Inheritance-Law-in-Tanzania1.*

Fleisch, Pail. *Lutheran Beginning Around Mt. Kilimanjaro.* Arusha: Makumira Publication. 1998.

Fontana, James. "Interviewing: The Art of Science". In N.K. Denzin and S. Yvonna, Lincojn. (eds), *Handbook of Qualitative Research.* Thousand Oaks: Sage, 1994.

Fiorenza, Elizabeth. *Discipleship of Equals: A Critical Feminist Ekklesia-logy of Liberation.* London: SCM Press Ltd, 1993.

———. Waiting-at-Table, a Critical Feminist Theological Reflection on Diakonia." *Concilium* 198 (1988): 84-94.

Fischman, Godson. *Imaging Teachers: Rethinking Gender Dynamics in Teacher Education.* Rowman and Littlefield Publishers, 2000.

Friedrich, Elena, and Cristina Trois. "Quantification of greenhouse gas emissions from waste management processes for municipalities–A comparative review focusing on Africa." *Waste management* 31, no. 7 (2011): 1585-1596.

Firdous, and Maheen Sultan, (eds). *Mapping Women's Empowerment: Experiences from Bangladesh, India and Pakistan.* Dhaka: University Press, 2010.

Bibliography

Gall, Gall, Borg. *Education Research: An Introduction*. Boston, Mass.: Allyn and Bacon, 2003.

Green, Todd. *Responding to Secularization: The deaconess Movement in Nineteenth-Century Sweden*. Boston: Brill, 2011.

Hoyle, Monica, Charles. *Research methods in social relations*. Thousand oaks California: Sage Publications, 2002.

Husu, Päivi. *Desire and Death: History through rituals practice in Kilimanjaro*. Helsinki: The Society, 1999.

Hugh, Richard. *Didascalia Apostolorum*. Oxford: Clarendon Press, 1922.

Jeaschke, Ernst. *Bruno Gutmann: His Life, His Thoughts and His Work*. Erlangen: Verlag der Ev. Luth. Mission, 1985.

Kanyoro, Musimbi R. A. and Robins Wendy, S. Editors. *The Power We Celebrate Women's Stories of Faith and Power*. Geneva: WCC Publications, 1992.

Karl, Marilee. *Women and Empowerment Participation and Decision Making*. London: Zed Books Ltd, 1995.

King, Ursula. *Feminist Theology from Third World: A Reader*. London: SPC/Orbis, 1994.

Kitange, Seth. *Huduma za Huruma: Hotuba na Maandiko Mbalimbali Kuhusu Diakonia katika Jamii na Kanisa*. Moshi. Moshi Lutheran Printing Press, 2003.

Kanyoro, Musimbi. *Introducing Feminist Cultural Hermeneutics*. Sheffiels: Sheffield Academic Press, 2002.

———. *The Power we Celebrate: Women's Stories of Faith and Power*. Sheffiels: Sheffield Academic Press, 1992.

Kothari, C. *Research Methodology; Methods and techniques*. Second Edition Revised. New Dehli: New Age International Publisher, 2005.

———. *Research Methodology; Methods and techniques*. Second Edition. New Dehli: New Age International Publisher, 2004.

Kvale, Svend. *Interviews. An introduction to Qualitative Research interviewing*. Thousand Oaks California: Sage Publications, 1996.

Kathleen, Stalhl, *History of the Chagga People of Kilimanjaro*. London.Mouton and Co, 1964.

Kurubai, R. M. "From Doubt to Acceptance: The Coming of Women into the Clerical Ministry in the – the Evangelical Lutheran Church in Tanzania (ELCT)." Master Thesis: University of Oslo, 2008.

Larson Bradford, Brown Mortimer, (Eds.) *Adolescents' preparation for the future—Perils and premises a report of the study group on adolescence in the 21st century*. Ann. Arbor: MI, 2002.

Lerner, Gerda. 'Why have there been so few women philosopher?" In Tougas, C. T. And Ebenreck, S. (eds). *Presenting women philosophers*. Philadelphia: Temple University Press. 2000.

Locke, Silverman, Spirduso, *Proposal that work: A guide for planning dissertations and grant proposals*. Thousand Oaks, Calif: Sage Publications, 2007.

Bibliography

Lyamuya, David. "The Ministry of the Church to HIV/AIDS orphans with the Reference to the ELCT, Northern Diocese East Kilimanjaro." *Unpublished MA dissertation, Makumira University College* (2003).

Mason, Carol. Feminist Waves, Feminist Generations: Life Stories from the Academy (review). *Journal on American Studies*. Volume 48 Number 2 (2007).

Mahanty Chandra. "Under Western Eyes". In Cutrufelli, M, R. *Women of Africa: The Roots of Oppressions*. London: Zed Books, 1983.

Mahmud, S. *Women's Empowerment and Reproductive change in rural Bangladesh*. Bangladesh: Bangladesh Institute of development studies, 2001.

Maanga, Godson. *Religion and Worldview in Chagga Traditional Religion. A Systematic Interpretation and a Theological Evaluation*. Master Thesis. Makumira University College, 2000.

Magesa, Laurent. *African Religion – The Moral traditions of Abundant Life*. Nairobi: Paulines Publications, 1997.

Majola, Aloo Osotsi. The Chagga Scapegoat Purification Rituals and another Re-reading of the Goat of Azazel in Leviticus 16. *Melita Theological* Vol.L.No1, 1999.

Marshal, Rossman. *Designing qualitative research*. Newbury park. Calif: Sage Publications, 1989.

Marshal, Rossman. *Designing qualitative research*. Newbury park. Calif: Sage Publications, 1998.

Markkola, Pirjo. The Calling of Women Gender, Religion and Social Reform in Finland, 1860–1920. In Markkola (Edt.). *Gender and Vocation: Women, Religion and Social Change in the Nordic Countries, 1830-1940*. Helsinki: Gummerus Printing, 2000.

Materu, John. "Christian Baptism in the Context of the Chagga Initiation Rites". Master Thesis: Norwegian School of Theology, 2007.

———. "The Impact of Chagga Traditional Belief and Practices on the Growth of Christian Faith". Bachelor Thesis. Makumira University College, 2002.

Merriam-Webster's online dictionary. *Patriarchy,* http://www.merriam-webster.com.

Moser Caroline. "Gender Planning in the Third World: Meeting Practicaland Strategic Gendered Needs' in World Development". http://www.popline.org/node/371962

Moore, Sally Falk. *Social Facts and Fabrications: "Customary" Law on Kilimanjaro, 1880-1980*. Cambridge: Cambridge University Press, 1986.

Moore, S. F. & Puritt, P. *The Chagga and Meru of Tanzania*. London: International African Institute, 1977.

Mushi, Philemon. *History and Development of Education in Tanzania*: Dar es Salaam University Press, 2009.

Mbiti, John. *Introduction to African Religion*. 2nd Edition Botswana:Heinemann Educational Publishers, 1991.

Bibliography

———. *Introduction to African Traditional Religion*. Heinemann. 1975.

McWhirter, Ellen. "Empowerment in Counselling". In Rowlands, J. *Questioning Empowerment: Working with Women in Honduras*. Oxford: Oxfam, 1991.

Mc Burney, Donald. *Research Methods*. 5 ed. India: Eastern Press Pvt. Ltd, 2003.

Mgossi, *Women's Economic Empowerment in Tanzania*, http://mgossi.blogspot.com/2011/12/womens-economic-empowerment-in-tanzania.html

Mwaura, Muiru, "Empowerment of Women: The Role of the Church". *Journal of African Christianity Thought*, Vol. 1, No.1, (1998).

Mwaluko G.M. *Health and Disease in Tanzania*. Published by Harper Collins Academic, 1991.

Mmbando, Paul, Kari A. Hartwig, Berit Hofgren, Phil DiSorbo, Shelley Smith, and Kristopher N. Hartwig. "Care for the most vulnerable children in Tanzania: a faith-based model of care and support for children affected by HIV." *Journal of health care for the poor and underserved* 20, no. 4A (2009): 13-21.

Nordstokke, Kjell . *Liberating Diakonia*. Trondheim: Tapir Akademisk Forlag, 2011.

———. "Empowerment in the perspective of ecumenical diakonia." *Diaconia* 3, no. 2 (2012): 185-195.

Oduyoye, Mercy. *Introducing African Women's Theology*. England: Sheffield Academic Press, 2001.

———. *Daughter of Anowa: African Women and Patriarch*. New York: Orbis Books, 2005.

———. "Reflections from the Third World Women's Experience and Liberation Theologies". In Fabella, V, and S. Torre (Eds.). *The Irruption of the Third World: Challenge to Theology: Papers from the fifth International Conference of the Ecumenical Association of Third World Theologians. August 17-29. New Delhi, India*. Maryknoll,NY: Orbis Books, 1983a.

———. "Feminist Theology in African Perspective". In Gibellini, R. (Ed.). *Paths of African Theology*. NY: Gruyter, 1994.

———. "Christian Feminism and African Culture: The Hearth of the Matter". In Ellis, M. & Maduro, M. (Eds.). *The Future Liberation Theology*. Maryknoll NY: Orbis Books, 1989.

———. *Who Will Roll the Stone Away?: The Ecumenical Decade of the Churches in Solidarity with Women*. Geneva: WCC, 1990.

———. *Introducing African Women's Theology*. England: Sheffield Academic Press, 2001.

Oduyeye, Mercy. and Kanyoro, M.R.A. *The Will to Rise: Women Traditions and the Church in Africa*. New York: Orbit Books, Mary Knoll, 1992.

Oftestad, Alf. *How to Build a Diaconal Church . A Short Introduction to The Biblical Understanding of Diakonia*. Diatekst, 2003.

Okure, T. *Women in the Bible. With Passion and Compassion: Third World Women Doing Theology: Reflections from the Women's Commission of ecumenical Association of Third World Theologians*. Maryknoll NY: Orbis Books, 1988.

Bibliography

Okure, T. Feminist Interpretations in Africa. In Schussler Fiorenza, E. (Ed.). *Searching the Scripture*. London: SCM Press, 1993.

Omari Cathbert. *Rural Women, Informal Sector and Household Economy in Tanzania*. Helsinki: World Institute for Development Economics Research, 1988.

Parmesan, Camille, and Gary Yohe. "A globally coherent fingerprint of climate change impacts across natural systems." *Nature* 421 (2003) 37-42.

Pemberton, Carie. *Circle Thinking: African Women Theologians in Dialogue with the West*. Boston: Brill Leiden, 2003.

Pessi, Anne Birgitta. The Churhch a a place of encounter: Communality and the Good life in Finland. In Backstrom, Anders and Davie, Grace. *Welfare and Religion in 21st Century Europe Volume 1*. Farnham: Ashgate, 2010.

Phiri, Isabel "Doing Theology as an African Woman". In Parratt, J (ed), *A Reader in African Theology*. London: SPCK, 1997.

Rasche, Ruth. "The Deaconess Sisters: Pioneer Professional Women." *Hidden Histories in the United Church of Christ* 1 (1984): 95-109.

Rai, Shirin. *Mainstreaming gender democratizing the state? Institutional mechanisms for the advancement of women*. Manchester. University Press, 2003.

Riipinen, Lilja K. (Ed). *Holy Deaconess: Aspects for the Diakonia Ministry in Asia*. Lite: Lutheran Institute of Theological Education, 2004.

Rose, P. and Tembon, M. "Girls and Schooling in Ethiopia". In Heward Ch. And Bunwaree, Sh. (Eds.). *Gender, Education and Development: Beyond Access to Empowerment*. London: Zed Books Ltd, 1999.

Rowlands, Jo. *Questioning Empowerment: Working with Women in Honduras*. Oxford: Oxfam, 1997.

Rogers, Joseph R. *My Role as a Deaconess*. Columbus: Brentwood Christian Press, 2011.

Robinson, Cecilia. *The Ministry of Deaconess*. U.S.A: CPSIA, 1898.

Rhoda, Chamshama, Emmanuel. "Prostitution, Culture And Church: A Study Of Gender Inequality In Chalinze, Tanzania." (2011).

Seitei, Gloria, T. "Areas of weaknesses, obstacles and challenges to economic empowerment of women in developing countries". In Prakash, N., Mclellan, B., and Weijnett, B. (Editors). *Empowerment of Women through sicience and technology interventions*. Delhi: Regency Publications, 2010.

Suzan, G. *Situating Fertility: Anthropology and Demographic Inquiry*. Cambridge: Cambridge University Press, 1995.

Sundkler, Bengt A. *A History of the Church in Africa*. United Kingdom: Cambridge University Press, 2000.

Stake, Richard and Wolcott, Harry. *The art of case study research*. Thousand Oaks, Calif: Sage Publications, 1994.

Shao, Martin. *Bruno Gutman's Missionary Method and Its Influence on the Evangelical Lutheran Church in Tanzani, Northern Diocese*. STM Thesis: Wartburg Theological Seminary, Dubuque Iowa, 1985.

Bibliography

Schwarz, Hans. *Beyond the Gates of Death: A Biblical Examination of Evidence for Life after Death*. Minneapolis: Augsburg Publishing House, 1981.

Schuler, Martin. *Empowerment and the law: Strategies of Third World Women*. Washington: McNaughton & Gunn, Inc,1986.

Stromquist, N.P. "The theoretical and practical bases for empowerment". In Anonuevo, C.M. (Ed.). *Women, Education and Empowerment: Pathways towards Autonomy*. Report of the International Seminar held at UIE, Hamburg 27 January–2 February 1993. Hamburg. 13- 22.

TANZANIA Country Report on the Millennium Development Goals 2010. Online at http://www.povertymonitoring.go.tz/WhatisNew/MDG%20Report%202010.pdf

Tong, Rosemarie. *Feminist Thought: a Comprehensive Introduction*. Colorado: Westview Press, 1989.

Tønnessen, Aud. "Changing Roles of Gender, Changing Roles of the Church". In Kunter, K. & Schjørring, J. H. (Editors.). *European and Global Christianity Challenges and Transformations in the 20th Century*. Arbeit: Vandenhoeck &Ruprecht, 2011. The Oxford Dictionary of the World Religion (1997).

Urio, Aaron. & Lema, Anzamen. "Ushirika wa Neema". In Kitange, S. (Editor.). *Huduma za Huruma: Hotuba na Maandiko Mbalimbali Kuhusu Diakonia katika Jamii na Kanisa*. Moshi. Moshi Lutheran Printing Press, 2003.

Urio, Aaron. "Kanisa na Huduma ya Udiakonia". In Ami, J.&Sævre, K.K. (Editors.). *Riziki*. Arusha. Scripture Mission, 2011.

UNFPA. "Understanding gender equality and women's empowerment". Online at http://www.unfpa.org/gender/empowerment.htm.

Ursula, King. *Feminist Theology from Third World: A Reader*. London: SPC/Orbis, 1994.

URT, *Tanzania Country Report on the Millennium Development Goal*. Dar es Salaam, 2010.

URT, Country *report on implementation of the beijing platform for action and the outcome document of the twenty-third special session of the general assembly- Beijing +10*. Dar es Salaam, 2005.

UNESCO, *Gender in Education Network in Asia-Pacific (GENIA) Toolkit: Promoting Gender Equality in Education*. Bangkok, 2009.

Vayrynen, Sai. *Evidence of empowerment: A study of Microfinance programs and women's empowerment in Kerala, India*. Master Thesis. The Norwegian University of Life Science (UMB), 2011.

Wijngaards, John. *Women Deacons in the Early Church: Historical Texts and Contemporary Debates*. New York: Crossroad Publishing Company, 2006.

Young, Iris Marion. *Throwing like a girl and other essays in feminist philosophy and social theory*. Bloomington: Indiana University Press, 1990.

Zanago, Phyllis. *Women in Ministry: Emerging Questions on the Diaconate*. Paulist Press, 2012.

www.ingramcontent.com/pod-product-compliance
Lightning Source LLC
Chambersburg PA
CBHW060821190426
43197CB00038B/2175